SECOND EDITION

Listen UP

Student Voices
on Critical Issues
and Values
in Real Life

Elisha J. Nixon-Cobb • Consuelo A. Bonillas

Kendall Hunt
publishing company

Cover image © Shutterstock, Inc.

Kendall Hunt
publishing company

www.kendallhunt.com
Send all inquiries to:
4050 Westmark Drive
Dubuque, IA 52004-1840

Copyright © 2008, 2011 by Kendall Hunt Publishing Company

ISBN 978-0-7575-9359-8

Printed in the United States of America
10 9 8 7 6 5 4 3 2

CONTENTS

LISTEN UP! STUDENT VOICES ON CRITICAL ISSUES
AND VALUES IN REAL LIFE, 2ND EDITION
ELISHA NIXON, PH.D., & CONSUELO BONILLAS, PH.D.

ABOUT THE AUTHORS

DR. ELISHA NIXON-COBB

Elisha Nixon-Cobb serves as program coordinator and professor in health education at Kean University in Union, New Jersey, in the Department of Physical Education, Health, Recreation, and Dance. She teaches courses in health education, including introduction to health, health counseling, women's health, minority health disparities, and courses in global studies.

Dr. Nixon-Cobb received her bachelor of arts degree in sociology from Geneva College, and her master's and doctorate in health education from The Pennsylvania State University. Nixon-Cobb has published several articles on critical thinking and an article on menopause in African-American women. Nixon-Cobb's current manuscript is titled *Multicultural Health Counseling*.

DR. CONSUELO BONILLAS

Consuelo Bonillas, an assistant professor in health education at Kean University, teaches courses in human sexuality, introduction to health, and health disparities and social justice.

Dr. Bonillas received her bachelor of arts degree in psychology from Mount Saint Mary's College in Los Angeles, her master's degree in social psychology from Syracuse University, and her doctorate in human sexuality education from Widener University in Chester, Pennsylvania. Dr. Bonillas has published articles on pregnancy, marriage equality, women's sexual and reproductive health, and sexual pleasure.

The authors have a combined total of 30 years of teaching, counseling, and research in the field of health education. It is both authors' belief that *Listen Up* must be grounded in both the female and male perspectives. For this reason, their courses, their students, and this text will benefit from an unbiased perception and deep appreciation of the importance of health and wellness.

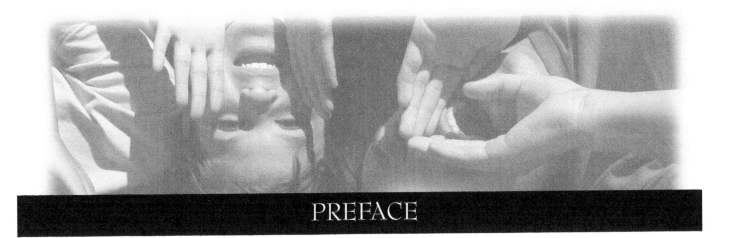

PREFACE

TO THE STUDENT

This textbook encourages you to live a healthier, more satisfying life. Knowledge gained, coupled with your ability to think critically about the choices you make, will impact your lifestyle now and in the future.

You are responsible for the decisions you make regarding your health. The various dimensions of your well-being will inevitably be affected by the decisions you make. Your decisions, which further your growth and understanding of who you are and why you do what you do, will also affect the nature of your relationships and your decisions about alcohol, drug, and tobacco use, as well as birth control, pregnancy, and abortion.

An important aspect of making healthy decisions is the ability to think critically before you act. Critical thinking is characterized as active, persistent, and careful consideration of any belief [or action]. . . (Dewey 1982, 74). In other words, questioning your actions before acting is an important aspect of the decision-making process.

This edition of *Listen Up: Student Voices on Critical Issues and Values in Real Life* not only includes real-life stories written by college students who dealt with their decisions or circumstances of life but also includes tools to assist you in thinking critically about your life changes. You will learn to identify the behavior, identify support for logic, evaluate the support or evidence, and lastly, evaluate the argument for or against maintain the behavior.

Making critical thinking part of your daily life is our challenge to you.

TO THE INSTRUCTOR

We write to challenge you to lead the way in instructing students in how to think critically about behavior change. Similar to the last edition, gaining knowledge about the importance of healthy behavior is the focus of this edition, but gaining basic health knowledge is not enough. Students must make a conscious decision to change, and we must make a conscious decision to teach them how to make healthy decisions that are sustainable through a lifetime.

To that end, this edition of *Listen Up* provides tools to enhance students' learning and instructors' teaching of critical thinking and behavior change. Key features of each chapter include vignettes filled with real-life examples of situations that are used in efforts to promote critical thinking and writing.

CHAPTER
1

Critical Thinking: A Building Block for Health

EXAMPLE

Casey is a senior expecting to graduate in the next few months. He is scheduled to take his first exam of the semester, but due to extenuating circumstances, he does not have time to read the material and take notes. In other words, Casey is totally unprepared to take his final exam. His closest friend recommends that he use a cheat sheet and sit close to him so he can show Casey the responses to his questions. In his heart of hearts Casey realizes that what his friend is asking him to do is wrong, but what other recourse does he have. Casey is also concerned about losing his best friend as well as failing his exam if he does not comply.

DEFINING CRITICAL THINKING

The previous example is a common issue that many students face at the beginning of the semester. Does Casey stand by his value system or accept the value system of others? What important questions should Casey consider? Should Casey examine his responses to the questions? Can he justify what he believes or says?

In response to Casey's dilemma, some students would not hesitate to provide a quick response. Other students would require more facts before making a decision.

Instead of thinking impulsively, "Thinking critically is an approach to thinking that's deliberate, purposeful, and organized in order to assess the value of information" (Smith 2000). To think critically, the information we draw on to make choices must also be assessed in an organized manner.

According to Chet Meyers in his book titled *Teaching Students to Think Critically*, critical thinking skills are content-specific. He further explains that critical thinking skills needed to critique art are not the same for chemistry or health sciences. Meyers suggest that instructors not treat critical thinking as a disjointed academic subject, and instead incorporate it throughout the subject of individual discipline (1986).

Other authors also suggest that there is not one single approach to the art of logic or critical thinking (Crowther & Allen 2006; Gardner, Jewler, & Cuseo 2000; Smith 2000). Instructors are encouraged to use their knowledge and wisdom in designing a stepwise approach to developing analytical skills that help students to determine the thesis statement or main message, identify the issue or problem and supporting information, and evaluate possible outcomes. A stepwise approach is also helpful in enhancing students' ability to discover inferences, biases, relationships, and cause and effect. Like Chet Meyers, a longtime supporter of critical thinking, the authors of *Listen Up* recommend short writing assignments spaced out throughout the semester that become increasingly complex with the application of various critical thinking skills, beginning with the less complex skills.

Another advocate of critical thinking is well-known educational psychologist, Benjamin Bloom. In 1956, Bloom identified six levels of cognitive development including knowledge, comprehension, application, analysis, synthesis, and evaluation—from simple recall or recognition of facts, as the lowest level of learning, to more complex and abstract levels of learning that require comprehension, analysis, synthesis, and evaluation (Bloom 1956). At the end of each chapter are questions designed to promote students' learning and enhance students' critical thinking skills.

BARRIERS TO CRITICAL THINKING FROM A STUDENT'S PERSPECTIVE

We all come with our own belief systems that can cause us to resist change or be challenged. Most students prefer rote learning assessments such as matching, multiple choice, and true/false questions, and they experience brain freeze when it comes to addressing essay questions. The following are some common barriers to critical thinking, as cited by several students:

1. There is not enough time to think through stuff.
2. If I think about changing a behavior, I also have to think about what to replace it with.
3. My instructor expects me to think, write, and pose questions at once.
4. My main task is to take notes, and think about what I've written later.

Instructors also have concerns about teaching students how to think critically.

BARRIERS TO CRITICAL THINKING FROM AN INSTRUCTOR'S PERSPECTIVE

Most instructors assume that students should know how to organize and assess their thinking long before entering college, and they experience disappointment when students' approaches to thinking do not meet expectations. As instructors, we have to spend some time training students to write, think, and argue inductively, while drawing on evidence from a shared body of knowledge. Without that foundation, it's harder to make—or demand from others—logical, informed decisions about managing their health. The following are common barriers to critical thinking, as cited by several instructors:

1. It's really not my job to teach students how to think and write critically. Didn't they take that in English 101?
2. Teaching students to think critically takes away from the content, which means I have to struggle to play catch-up.
3. By the time I instruct students how to evaluate their thinking, most express very little interest in applying what they learned to the content.

HOW TO PROMOTE CRITICAL THINKING IN THE CLASSROOM

Before students can truly share their thoughts, they need to begin listening to one another—in other words, they need to get out of the habit of gazing at and directing almost all their comments to the instructor. To facilitate dialogue, have the students sit in a circle instead of traditional seating and give each student a 5 foot by 9 inch ruled or unruled index card, asking them to fold the card lengthwise and write their names in bold with a marker that is passed around the room. Afterward, instruct students to position the name card in such a way that it hangs over the edge of the desk and is visible to all in the classroom.[1] The instructor can collect the name cards after each class and return to students at the beginning of class to avoid having to provide another index card to students who misplace their name tags.

Creating a supportive classroom environment is another effective strategy for promoting critical thinking. Students are told that if the class is to create a supportive and effective learning environment, they must show respect for others and speak only when called on. The instructor may need to emphasize that she/he will intermittently share new information or pose questions, but it is the students' responsibility to keep the conversation going.

---

[1] The idea of using name tags and having students call on each other to participate is a strategy Elisha Nixon learned from Dr. Michael Johnson of the Sociology Department at Pennsylvania State University, with whom she team-taught a course about racism and sexism in the United States.

When a student responds to a question, she is responsible for turning toward another student whose hand is raised and call on him by name to respond. If no one has a hand raised after a comment is made, the student can still call on a student who appears to be listening attentively (whether by nodding in agreement or by looking skeptical or puzzled).

Removing the professor from the "all-knowing" position to the position of facilitator promotes communication among students, and having students call on each other by name helps to establish a sense of intimacy and community. Initially, of course, the instructor may need to prompt students who have just spoken to look around the room to notice the raised hands or engaged expressions of peers (Byrd & Nixon et al. 2010).

Shy students can choose another alternative to oral participation. Students who are reluctant to share their thoughts out loud can choose to write two-page summaries and reactions to what they read for points that, when totaled, equal the same as oral participation.

Creating approaches to critical thinking takes time, patience, and attention to classroom exercises and assignments that force students to practice critical thinking. In the following chapters, the authors provide practical suggestions for helping students apply critical thinking skills beginning with the memory of previously learned material by recalling facts, terms, basic concepts to form a simple topic sentence and thesis statement and building toward more complex critical thinking skills.

REFLECTION

Critical thinking does not develop naturally as students learn more complex information. The ability to analyze a modern novel, business strategy, as well as health behaviors must be taught intentionally, with clarity. Since learning to think critically does not occur in a vacuum, students must learn to familiarize themselves with the reading, including key concepts and issues that come alive or have more meaning when coupled with the students' and instructors' real-life experiences.

CRITICAL THINKING QUESTIONS

1. From time to time, everyone experiences some kind of barrier(s) to logical critical thinking. List and briefly discuss barriers to your ability to think during a test or when participating in open class discussion.
2. Identify and briefly discuss your most proficient level of critical thinking.
3. Discuss the relationship between critical thinking and healthy behavior change.

REFERENCES

Bloom, B. (1956). *Taxonomy of educational objectives: The classification of educational goals: Handbook I. Cognitive domain.* London: Longmans, Green.

Byrd, D., Nixon, E., Beckman, E., McMahon, E., Seetch, B., & Smith, A. (2010). *Teaching troubles: classroom strategies for confronting power and privilege.* Baltimore, Maryland: Institute for Teaching and Research on Women.

Crowther, A., & Allen, J. (2006). *The daily spark: Critical writing-warm-up exercises.* Canada: Spark Publishing.

Gardner, J., Jewler, J., & Cuseo, J. (2000). *Our college experience: Strategies for success.* Belmont, Calif.: Wadsworth.

Meyers, C. (1986). *Teaching students to think critically.* San Francisco, Calif.: Jossey-Bass Publishers.

Smith, B. D. (2000). *Bridging the gap.* New York: Addison Wesley Longman, Inc.

CHAPTER

2

Introduction to Health and Wellness

1. Define health and wellness.
2. Explain the dimensions of health and wellness.
3. Recall factors that influence behavior change.
4. Discuss the health belief model.
5. Discuss the influence of race and culture on health.
6. Apply critical thinking skill Level 1, Knowledge.

HEALTH AND WELLNESS

Most of us can rise early in the morning to shower, eat breakfast, and dress ourselves without difficulty, while others may need assistance. Are individuals who need assistance to cross the street or lift a spoon to feed ourselves or get dressed in the morning healthy? Based on the World Health Organization (WHO) definition of health, individuals with physical or mental disabilities can lead healthy and active lives. According to WHO (1947), *health* means being sound in body, mind, and spirit. "Health is not merely the absence of disease or infirmity, but "a state of complete physical, mental, and social well-being." Maintaining one's health is a process by which men and women learn how to maintain or change behaviors that have the potential to positively transform our bodies, minds, and spirits, and thus encourage others.

Wellness, a relatively new term, is defined as "the adaptation of healthy lifestyle habits that will enhance well-being while decreasing the risk of disease." The "well" person is not necessarily the strong, the brave, the successful, the young, or whole, or even the illness-free being, notes John Travis, M. D., author of the *Wellness Workbook*. "No matter what your current state of health, you can bring to appreciate yourself as a growing, changing person and allow yourself to move toward a happier life and positive health" (Travis & Ryan, in Hales 2011).

HEALTH: A MULTIDIMENSIONAL PARADIGM

As evidence in the concepts of health and wellness, the structure and function of the body includes an array of activities, all of which are interconnected to seven components or dimensions of health (see Figure 2.1).

PHYSICAL DIMENSION (BODY)

Ensuring good physical health begins with devoting attention and time to attaining healthy levels of cardiovascular fitness, muscular strength and endurance, flexibility, and body composition. When coupled with good nutritional practices, good sleep habits, and the avoidance of risky social behaviors such as drinking and driving or unprotected sexual intercourse, a physically fit and healthy body results. This is the component of health most associated, at first glance, with a person's health.

EMOTIONAL HEALTH (FEELINGS)

An individual who is emotionally healthy is able to enjoy life despite unexpected challenges and problems. Effectively coping with life's difficulties and unexpected events is essential to maintaining good health. Equally important to good personal wellness is the ability to understand your feelings and express those feelings or emotions outwardly in a positive and constructive manner. Negative emotions that stay trapped on the inside of us can affect the

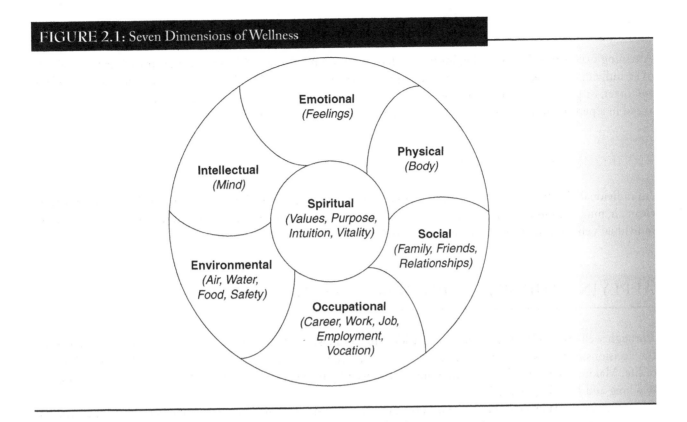

immune system and result in chronic stress, which can lead to serious illness such as diabetes, high blood pressure, and cardiovascular disease.

SOCIAL HEALTH (FAMILY, FRIENDS, RELATIONSHIPS)

Social health is an individual's ability to relate to and interact with others. Socially healthy people are able to communicate and interact with other people they come in contact with each day. They are respectful and caring of their family, neighbors, and associates. Although reaching out and communicating with others might be difficult or uncomfortable at times, it is extremely important to a person's social health and overall sense of well-being.

INTELLECTUAL HEALTH (MIND)

Among some African cultures, there is the belief that where the mind goes, the body will follow. The mind can have substantial influence over the body. To be intellectually healthy, it is essential to continue to explore new avenues and interests and to regularly engage in new and ongoing learning opportunities and experiences. Uncomfortable as it may be, the more unknowns an individual faces or explores, the more opportunity she or he has to learn and grow intellectually.

SPIRITUAL HEALTH (VALUES, PURPOSE, INTUITION, AND VITALITY)

The spiritual aspect helps us to achieve a sense of inner peace, satisfaction, and confidence. It can help give us hope and a sense that all is right with the world. An individual's ethics, values, beliefs, and morals can contribute to their spiritual health. Good spiritual health can also help give meaning and purpose to one's life.

OCCUPATIONAL HEALTH

Attaining occupational wellness begins with determining what roles, activities, and commitments take a majority of an individual's time. These roles, activities, or commitments could include but are not limited to being a student, volunteer, or part-time employee while pursuing one's degree. It is when each of the areas are integrated and balanced in a personally and professionally fulfilling way that occupational wellness occurs.

ENVIRONMENTAL HEALTH (SURROUNDINGS)

An individual's health and wellness can be substantially affected by the quality of his or her environment. Access to clean air, nutritious food, clean water, and adequate clothing and shelter are essential components to being well. An individual's environment should, at the very least, be clean and safe.

APPLYING THE SEVEN DIMENSIONS OF WELLNESS

Through wellness, an individual manages a wide range of lifestyle choices. How individuals choose to behave and the decisions they make in each of the seven dimensions of health and wellness will determine their overall quality of life. Making an active effort to combining and constantly trying to balance each of the seven dimensions is key to a long and fulfilling life.

Our health is in a constant state of flux or change. The decision to change or reduce negative behaviors that have the potential to affect all dimensions of health is dependent on what types of beliefs and values provide the best explanation of why we do what we do.

FACTORS THAT INFLUENCE HEALTH

Personal heath is influenced by several major factors, including heredity, environment, personal behavior, and access to health care services (Floyd, Mimms, & Yelding 2008). Behavior change does not occur by itself. Factors that influence behavior change can be divided into three general categories: predisposing, enabling, and reinforcing.

1. *Predisposing factors.* Our life experiences, knowledge and cultural experiences, and current beliefs and values act to predispose or influence behavior. Examples of factors that predispose us to certain conditions include age, race, ethnicity, family background, and educational background. For example, if your parents engaged in drug behavior that put them at risk, there is a 90 percent greater chance of your participating in risky drug behavior than someone whose parents didn't. If your peers participate in risky drug behavior, there is an 80 percent greater chance you will do the same than someone whose friends don't.
2. *Enabling factors.* Your skills and abilities, physical, emotional, and mental capabilities are enabling factors. They reflect the ease or difficulty with which individuals commit to making health decisions. Positive enablers can work in your favor, while negative enablers can sabotage your success.
3. *Reinforcing factors.* The presence or absence of support and encouragement can derail one's present and future aspirations. For example, if you decide to go to college and family members continue to devalue a college education or your potential to succeed in college, your failure or lack of confidence in your potential is reinforced.

However, most individuals have been in situations in which predisposing, enabling, and reinforcing factors have negatively impacted their lives, and yet these individuals were able to overcome life's obstacles and lead productive purposeful life.

The Health Belief Model provides an explanation of how an individual's attitudes and beliefs can predict health behaviors.

THE HEALTH BELIEF MODEL

The Health Belief Model (HBM) was developed by a group of investigators associated with U.S. Public Health Services from 1950 to 1960 to explain and predict health behaviors based on an individual's attitude and beliefs (Green & Morton-Simmons 1984; Hales 2011; Floyd, Mimms, & Yelding 2008).

Individuals must be ready to act on their beliefs dependent on how realistic the goal, their level of self-efficacy or confidence, the benefits expected, and cues to action. The following four categories of beliefs offer strong support as to whether or not one will take action to prevent or reduce negative behavior, with specific examples:

1. *Perceived seriousness.* Individuals who do not view unwanted pregnancy, HIV/AIDS, etc. as serious usually will not have a positive response to birth control or safe sex.
2. *Perceived susceptibility.* An individual's perceptions of the likelihood of becoming pregnant or contracting HIV may affect his or her willingness to take prevention action.
3. *Perceived benefits.* For the most part, an individual's desire for instant gratification is a determinant of whether or not a health action will actually do some good. Individuals who are bent on immediately receiving something in return may very well view behavior change as a waste of time.
4. *Perceived barriers.* Individuals may perceive the task of trying to reduce or eliminate a negative behavior as too difficult. The notion that behavior change is too difficult or impossible is usually coupled with the possible consequences. In other words, the cost of maintaining healthy behavior change such as ending alcohol abuse might be too steep a price to pay.

DO RACE AND CULTURE MATTER?

Epidemiology is the study of the distribution and determinates of mortality (death) and morbidity (illness) in human populations. Behavior change theories have been effective in improving an individual's overall health. Despite improvements, there are American citizens—including African Americans, American Indians, Hispanics, Latinos, and Pacific Islanders—who, compared to Caucasians, suffer poor health and die prematurely. The life expectancy for black women is 3.7 years shorter compared to white women, and for black men is 5.6 years shorter compared to white men (CDC 2011). Contributing factors include poverty, genetics, lack of education, environmental influences, and specific health behaviors resulting in delay in treatment.

How do race and culture affect health status? Among Hispanics, Puerto Ricans suffer disproportionately from asthma, while Mexican Americans have higher rates for diabetes. Black Americans lose substantially more years of potential life to homicide (nine times as many), and stroke and diabetes (three times as many) as whites. Caucasians are prone to skin cancer and osteoporosis and metabolic disorders that can lead to mental retardation.

Native Americans are more likely to die young primarily as a result of accidental injuries, cirrhosis, and complications of diabetes (Baltimore American College Health Association 2010).

As indicated, maternal and infant mortality and morbidity rates are key determinants of health, as well as prevalence (existing cases) and incidence rates (new cases) and life expectancy (expectation of life) (LaVeist 2005).

REFLECTION

Health behavior change does not occur in a vacuum. Long-term behavior change requires movement through many stages, with access to positive support systems that enable us to lead meaningful lives and provide hope to the next generation.

CRITICAL THINKING SKILL

Level 1, Knowledge. Exhibit memory of previously learned material by recalling facts, terms, basic concepts, and answers.

Bloom's Taxonomy Key Words. Count, define, list, match, name, outline, recall, state, write, identify.

CRITICAL THINKING QUESTIONS FOR LEVEL 1, KNOWLEDGE

1. Write a thesis sentence using concepts and ideas from today's readings.
2. Identify at least one predisposing, reinforcing, and enabling factor that has influenced your health attitudes and/or behaviors.
3. After talking to three classmates from different racial or ethnic backgrounds about their health attitudes and behaviors, what key facts, terms, or basic concepts can you recall from today's readings that relate to the health information shared by classmates?

WEBSITES

www.cdc.gov

Stay up to date on the latest public health news and the Centers for Disease Control newsletter and recommendations for protecting your health.

http://medlineplus.gov

Medline contains links to information on hundreds of health conditions and issues.

www.WebMD.com

This website is full of information to help you manage your health. The site also has quizzes and calculators to test your knowledge of health in a fun way.

REFERENCES

Baltimore American College Association (2010). *Reference Group Executive Summary, 2009.*

Floyd, P., Mimms, S., & Yelding, C. (2008). *Personal health: Perspectives and lifestyles.* Belmont, Calif: Thomson Wadsworth.

Green, W., & Morton-Simmons, B. (1984). *Introduction to health education.* New York: Macmillan.

Hales, D. (2012). *An invitation to health*. Belmont, CA: Wadsworth.

LaVeist, T. (2005). *Minority populations and health: An introduction to health disparities in the U.S.* San Francisco, Calif.: Jossey-Bass.

Prochaska, J. (1994). *Changing for good*. New York: Quill.

Travis, J., & Ryan, R. S. (2004). *The wellness workbook* (3rd ed.). Berkley, Calif.: Celestial Arts.

WHO (World Health Organization). "Constitution of the World Health Organization." *Chronicle of WHO 1* (1947), 1.

CHAPTER
3

Wellness and Stress

ARE YOU STRESSED: HOW DO YOU KNOW?

What do you do when you are stressed? Some people eat more. You might experience headaches or become more irritable than usual, tired, or anxious. Most individuals have a collection of symptoms that, if not put in check, can cause disease or illness. *Stress* refers to the physiological and psychological responses to unexpected change in our lives.

On the one hand, pleasant stress that results from pleasant events such as getting engaged, studying and getting an A on the final, and speaking before receiving an award are examples of *eustress*. Events that produce eustress are usually events that enhance our self-esteem and self-efficacy. On the other hand, stress resulting from unpleasant events that many students experience as a result of test anxiety, speech anxiety, learning problems, homesickness, relationship problems, and procrastination and others is referred to as *distress*.

The body's response to the stressful symptoms we experience is referred to as the *general adaptation syndrome* (GAS) (Payne, Hahn, & Lucas 2006).

THE GENERAL ADAPTATION SYNDROME

When stressed, an individual's body responds in predictable ways. For example, when asked to give a speech, maybe your heart rate increases, your speech pattern becomes pressured or tense, your throat becomes dry, and your palms and/or underarms sweat. According to Hans Selye (1984), the body moves through three stages when confronted by stressors: (1) alarm, (2) resistance, and (3) exhaustion.

THE ALARM STAGE

When exposed to a threatening event, the body immediately prepares to deal with the physiological and psychological changes that take place. To deal with these changes, the body enters the alarm stage. The body's physical reactions to stressful events include decreased digestive activity, increased metabolic rate, increased sweating, increased muscular tension, increased cardiac function, increased fat metabolism, and decreased clotting time (Payne, Hahn, & Lucas 2006).

RESISTANCE STAGE

During the second stage of the general adaptation syndrome, the body attempts to gain its internal balance or equilibrium. Because the body wants to survive, staying in the alarm phase is not conducive to one's well-being. So the body will do all that it can to reduce the intensity of the threat. During the resistance stage, specific organ systems such as the cardiovascular and digestive systems will begin to slow down. As a result, you will find yourself calming down and breathing a bit easier in an attempt to relieve the stress.

EXHAUSTION STAGE

In the exhaustion stage, individuals (as indicated) feel exhausted, as if they have been in a physical and emotional battle. As they gain more control over their bodily functioning, they can begin to recover the stress. The speed at which you recover from a stressful situation will determine the negative effect that the stressor will have on your body.

HOW DOES STRESS MANIFEST ITSELF?

Stress can manifest itself in four ways:
1. Emotionally
   - Do you always feel rushed, without enough time to get all that is needed done well or done at all?
   - Do you find it difficult to relax?
   - Are you irritable and moody, or easily angered?
   - Do you feel helpless or hopeless?
   - Do you want to cry for no apparent reason?
   - Is it difficult for you to listen or pay attention to your friends without being distracted?
   - Is it hard for you to fall asleep even on days you are exhausted?
   - When you do fall asleep, is it difficult to stay asleep?
2. Mentally
   - Are you indecisive in many areas of your life?
   - Is it difficult for you to concentrate?
   - Do you regularly have bad dreams or nightmares?
   - Do you have negative thoughts, including suicidal thoughts?
3. Behaviorally
   - Has your appetite changed so that you have gained or lost significant amounts of weight?
   - Are you neglecting yourself/your appearance?
   - Have you curtailed social activities?
   - Have you taken to substance abuse—i.e., cigarette smoking, drug use, or excessive alcohol or coffee intakes?
4. Physically
   - Do you have an increased heart rate or blood pressure?
   - Can you feel your own heart beat?
   - Do you feel out of breath or have tightness in your chest?
   - Do you suffer from frequent headaches or muscle aches due to chronic tension?
   - Is it difficult for you to digest food—leading to nauseousness or diarrhea?
   - Do you suffer from frequent attacks of infections such as influenza or sore throats?

Stress is not the cause of illness, but when it goes on for long periods of time or is particularly irritating it can become harmful by weakening an individual's immune system and increasing that person's risk of getting sick. There are a number of ways to control stress. However, what works for one person will not necessarily be helpful to someone else. It is important to recognize the stressor and determine the most effective way(s) to relieve, reduce, or eliminate that particular stressor. Another key to successfully managing stressors is to use a strategy that produces positive results, rather than a strategy that creates additional stress in an individual's life. Also, to be successful with stress management, give a particular stressor only the amount of energy it warrants—do not give a "10 cent stressor $10 worth" of time or energy. The following are general tips that help maintain a healthy lifestyle and can prepare an individual to cope with many of the stressors found in everyday life.
1. Deal with the cause:
   Finish the task, talk to the person, fix the tire, write the letter, make the call—do what needs to be done to deal with the situation. The longer a situation gets put off, the more stress it can create.

2. Put the situation into perspective:

How important is it really? How important will this be tomorrow, in six months? Most situations that tax physical/mental energies will soon be inconsequential and forgotten. Determine if anything can be done about the situation, or is it a situation that calls for acceptance?

3. Pace yourself:

No one can be in "high gear" all the time. Too often individuals stop to "smell the roses" only after the first accident or heart attack. Set short and intermediate goals—reward yourself upon reaching these goals.

4. Laugh at life and at yourself:

Humor is a wonderful tool. Laughing is internal jogging! She or he who laughs . . . lasts! See the humor in people and the absurdity of situations. Read the "funny pages."

5. Develop quality relationships:

Seek social and emotional support systems—individuals who care, love, and will listen to you. Express feelings constructively. Be there for others and allow others to be there for you in the good times and in the bad times.

6. Time management needs to be life management:

Look at goals and responsibilities from a bigger perspective; this can help with decision making. Streamline activities by breaking big, imposing jobs into small components. Seek assistance when it is needed; don't try to do everything yourself.

7. Look at situations and people in a different light—try an attitude adjustment:

Is your perception of the situation, event, or person correct? Is there another way to handle things, or is there another possible way to answer the problem? Go easier on yourself and on others. It is unreasonable to expect perfection from yourself or from others. Perfection is a "moving target" and causes constant stress. Take care of the things you can; don't worry about the things that are beyond your control.

8. Balance fun and responsibility:

Family, society, and community encourage and command constant work and responsibility. It is important to contribute and to meet responsibilities, but it is also important to find enjoyment and fun in life as well. Do something you find enjoyable on a regular basis and don't feel guilty!

9. Exercise and eat sensibly:

Exercise is one of the best stress-busters. Schedule exercise into your life. Walk, bike, swim, stretch, and recreate. Good food in proper proportions is also essential to good health and is an excellent way to reduce the negative effects stress may have on your life.

EFFECTIVE COPING STRATEGIES

Our body talks to us in many ways. If you listen closely, your body will let you know when you are in a state of imbalance. So here are some effective ways of managing the body's need for relief from stress.

NUTRITION

Some of us tend to overeat in order to cope with the stressors in our lives. Typically, eating high-sugar and high-fat foods such as chips, cookies, candy, or heaping servings of fried chicken and fries or, alternatively, not eating enough is not the best way to handle stress. Eating too much or too little can lead to serious health problems, such as obesity, eating disorders, diabetes, and hypertension (Payne, Hahn, & Lucas 2006).

SLEEP

Sleeping too much or too little is also an ineffective way to manage stress. Sleeping too much can result in increased depression and decreased energy levels. Seven to eight hours of sleep a night is recommended for optimal stress recovery time.

EXERCISE

Exercise is a great stress reliever. By tensing and releasing the muscles through exercise, you are allowing your body to relax and unwind. Endorphins released during exercise help to counter stress and reduce pain.

OTHER STRESS RELIEVERS

Positive self-talk can have a tremendous effect on how well you manage stress. Sometimes we can work ourselves into a frenzy by worrying or imagining the worst. Sometimes our worrying can cause unnecessary stress that can lead to ill health (McGinnis 1990).

Completing tasks in a timely manner can reduce stress. Some individuals who are habitual procrastinators perceive prolonging the completion of a task until the last minute as an effective coping strategy. In fact, they may very well get the job done on time, but what shape are they in physically and psychologically after the task is completed?

Having a sense of humor about some of the dumb things we do that at the time makes sense also helps. Being able to laugh at yourself is healthy. Laughing releases dopamine and endorphins that help us to relax. Add the act of laughing with a good friend and you will find that what caused discomfort and distress can actually turn out to enhance your well-being.

REFLECTION

Often, we are not aware of the toll that chronic stress can take on our physical and psychological well-being. Studies indicate that chronic stress can rob us of important nutrients, damage the cardiovascular system, raise blood pressure, and weaken the immune system, leaving us vulnerable to preventable infections and disease. Although much is known about stress and its causes, most individuals are only beginning to understand the nature of stress and its potential to do good or harm.

CRITICAL THINKING SKILL

Level 1, Knowledge. Exhibit memory of previously learned material by recalling facts, terms, basic concepts, and answers.

Bloom's Taxonomy Key Words. Count, define, list, match, name, outline, recall, state, write, identify.

CRITICAL THINKING QUESTIONS FOR LEVEL 1, KNOWLEDGE

1. Define stress in your own words and identify the stressors in your life that might put you at risk for chronic stress that could lead to illness and disease.
2. Compare and contrast distress and eustress and provide examples that are not indicated in the text.
3. Discuss the three stages of the general adaptation syndrome and distinguishing roles of each stage.
4. How does stress relate to your physical and psychological health?

WEBSITES

http://www.iienetwork.org

This website provides insight as to the stressors that international students experience as they move from one culture to another.

REFERENCES

McGinnis, L. (1990). *The power of optimism.* New York: Harper & Row.

Payne, W., Hahn, D., & Lucas, E. (2006). *Understanding your health* (9th ed.). New York: McGraw-Hill.

Selye, H. (1984). *The stress of life.* New York: McGraw-Hill.

CHAPTER 4

Violence and Abuse

1. Identify and discuss societal and personal factors that contribute to violence.
2. Discuss violence in families.
3. Summarize the prevalence of and factors contributing to sexual violence.
4. Discuss the way men respond to female-perpetrated violence.
5. Apply critical thinking skill Level 2, Comprehension.

VIOLENCE IN THE UNITED STATES

It's hard to pick up a newspaper or watch television without seeing evidence of violence. Reports of robberies, gang-related violence, murder, domestic violence, and rape are commonplace. The term *violence* indicates a set of behaviors that produce unintentional (committed without intent to harm) or intentional (committed with intent to harm) consequences. Regardless of the intent, violence always includes force.

Violence has always been a major concern in the United States. In 1985, the United States Public Health service identified violence as a leading health problem that contributes to death and disability.

The most violent-prone years of life are between the ages of 10 to 24, with 70.8 percent of all deaths during that time having violent elements. For ages 15 to 44, motor vehicles crashes (particularly when alcohol is involved), other unintentional injuries, homicide, and suicide are the most common violent contributors of death (Centers for Disease Control and Prevention 2008).

FACTORS RELATED TO VIOLENCE

The causes of violence are multifaceted. Violence can be related to stress of one kind or another. When stressors are uncomfortable, unpredictable, or chronic, the likelihood of substance abuse increases (Anisman & Merali 1999). According to Coker et al. (2000), alcohol and drug may very well contribute to violent behavior. One study conducted by the preceding found that male partners' unemployment and drug or alcohol use were associated with increased risk for physical, sexual, and/or emotional abuse.

Unplanned pregnancies can also cause emotional stress and strain where women report being the victims of beatings before and after childbirth (Jasinski 2004). Unemployment and poverty can also increase the likelihood of violence. Low socioeconomic and poor living conditions can create an environment of hopelessness in which some people view violence as the only way to obtain what they want (Donatelle 2010).

Discrimination, when one group is oppressed or perceives that its members are oppressed by another group, can breed discontent, and violence against others is more likely (Donatelle 2010).

VIOLENCE AND THE FAMILY

Although the family is based on love among its members, the way it is organized encourages conflict (Gelles and Straus 1979, 1988; Rouse, 1997). Like most social organizations, the family is a power system—meaning that power is unequally distributed between parents and children and between spouses, with the male parent typically dominant.

SOCIAL ORGANIZATION AND VIOLENCE IN THE FAMILY

Male dominance is perpetuated by the legal system and religious teachings. When male dominance is threatened, it's often resisted through violence. Also, parents have authority over their children, and therefore feel they have a right to punish children in some manner in order to shape them in ways parents consider important. Marriage, too, can become a battleground for power and control. This dynamic may not be operative in your home where there is a basic agreement on gender roles, but for many couples where there is an imbalance of power, these issues are a constant source of stress (Zinn, Eitzen, Wells 2011). Gelles and Strauss (1988) summarize the importance of this dimension for understanding family violence:

> The greater the inequity, the more one person makes all the decisions and has all the power, the greater the risk of violence. Power, power confrontations, and perceived threats to domination, in fact, are underlying issues in almost all acts of family violence. (82)

In addition, family privacy enhances the likelihood of violence. The rule in our society that the home is private has two negative consequences. First, it insulates family members from the protection that society can provide if another family member becomes abusive. Second, privacy often prevents the victims of abuse from seeking outside help.

EFFECT OF MEDIA VIOLENCE ON THE FAMILY

Family members are capable of interpersonal violence as well. Family violence is the use of force by one family member against another, with the intent to hurt, inure, or cause harm. Violent behavior is glorified in the movies and on television. The total number of violent acts children view on television over the course of their childhood is staggering. The American Psychiatric Association calculates that by age 18, the average American child will have seen 16,000 simulated murders and 200,000 acts of violence (Brown & Bzostek 2003).

Many studies link exposure to media violence and negative outcomes. Research findings indicate increased aggressive attitudes and behaviors, fears, and desensitization to violence correlated with exposure to media violence. In fact, children who identify with aggressive television characters have been found to be more likely to be aggressive as adults. In addition increased depression, nightmares, and sleep disturbances are associated with viewing media violence (Brown & Bzostek 2003).

RAPE AND OTHER SEXUAL VIOLENCE

Ideally, sexual intimacy is a mutual, enjoyable form of communication between two people. Far too often, though, one or both persons in a relationship will behave in an aggressive and hostile manner. Victims of rape and sexual assault can be young, old, male, or female.

In recent years, closer attention has been paid to victims of sexual assault that occurs during intimate relationships. Acquaintance rape refers to forced sexual intercourse between two individuals who know each other. Date rape is a form of acquaintance rape that involves forced sexual intercourse by a dating partner. Studies on college campuses suggest that about 20 percent of college women have experienced date rape, but a recent report issued by the Bureaus of Justice Statistics puts the figure at 3 percent per year. This figure includes completed and attempted rapes (Fisher, Cullen, & Turner 2001).

Sexual harassment, by contrast, is defined as unwanted attention of a sexual nature, including unwanted physical contact, excessive pressure for dates, sexually explicit humor, sexual innuendos or remarks, offers of job advancement based on sexual favors, and overt sexual assault (Hahn, Payne, and Lucas 2011).

PREVALENCE OF DATING VIOLENCE

Physical and sexual victimization are serious problems affecting young women in high school and college. In a study conducted by White and Ross (2003), results indicated that 32 percent of the 1,569 college-age women who completed five surveys during their four years in college experienced physical dating violence from age 14 through their college years (the average age of the women was 21.4 years).

The National Longitudinal Study of Adolescent Health conducted by Halpen et al. (2001) employed a nationally representative sample of nearly 7,000 high school students and found that 10 percent of the young women reported having been pushed by a romantic partner in the 18 months before the survey, and 3 percent reported having something thrown at them by their partner.

FACTORS THAT AFFECT VICTIMIZATION

The group of women most likely to be physically or sexually victimized or covictimized across the four years of college were those with a history of both childhood victimization (any type) and physical victimization in adolescence. Women who were physically victimized in adolescence but not in childhood were the group at second greatest risk. Higher proportions of this group of women experienced subsequent victimization than of women who were victimized in childhood but not in adolescence. The group at lowest risk were those who experienced neither childhood nor adolescent victimization (Smith, White, & Holland 2003).

MEN AS VICTIMS; WOMEN AS PERPETRATORS

Are men also victims of domestic violence? Some women do abuse and even kill their partners. The difference between male and female batters is twofold: First, although the frequency of physical aggression may be similar, the impact is drastically different: Women are injured in domestic incidents two to three times more often than men (National Coalition Against Domestic Violence 2007). These injuries tend to be more severe and have resulted in significantly more deaths. Second, a woman who is physically abused by a man is generally intimidated by him: She fears that he will use his power and control over her in some fashion. Men, however, generally report that they do not live in fear of their wives, even if the wife is abusive (Donatelle 2010).

REFLECTION

Violence affects us all, regardless of race, class, or gender. Avoiding difficult situations or learning to be vigilant during times in which harm is more likely to result may be our best defense in preventing violence.

CRITICAL THINKING SKILL

Level 2, Comprehension. Demonstrate understanding of facts and ideas by organizing, comparing, translating, interpreting, giving descriptions, and stating main ideas.

Blooms Taxonomy Key Words. Compare, extend, rephrase, contrast, associate, discuss, explain, rewrite, summarize, and provide examples.

CRITICAL THINKING QUESTIONS FOR LEVEL 2, COMPREHENSION

1. What facts or ideas in this chapter provide support for Gelles and Straus's statement regarding the cause(s) of violence?
2. State or interpret in your own words the impact of domestic violence perpetrated by males toward women and violence perpetrator by females toward men.
3. In your opinion, what can men and women do to reduce the incidence of violence, particularly sexual assault?

WEBSITES

http://www/childwelfare.gov

The U.S. Department of Health and Human Services has a clearinghouse on child abuse and neglect, called the Child Welfare Information Gateway.

http://www.dvalianza.org

The National Latino Alliance for the Elimination of Domestic Violence provides information to help address family violence.

http://www.dahmw.org

The Domestic Abuse Helpline for Men and Women is at the forefront of providing crisis intervention and support to victims of intimate personal violence.

REFERENCES

Anisman, H., & Merali, Z. (1999). Understanding stress: Characteristics and caveats. *Alcohol Research and Health, 23*, 241–249.

Brown, B., & Bzostek, S. *Violence in the lives of children*. Child Trends Data Bank Publication #2003-15. Online: http://www.childrensdatabank.org.

Coker, A. L., McKeown, R. E., Sanderson, M., Davis, K. E., Valois, R. F., & Huebner, E. S. (2000). Severe dating violence and quality of life among South Carolina high school students. *American Journal of Preventive Medicine, 19*, 220–227.

Donatelle, R. (2010). *Access to health*. San Francisco: Benjamim Cummings.

Fisher, B. S., Cullen, F. T., & Turner, M. G. (2001). *The sexual victimization of college women*. U.S. Department of Justice, Bureau of Justice Statistics, NCJ 182369. Washington, DC.

Gelles, R., & Straus, M. (1979). Determinants of violence in the family. In *Contemporary theories about the family*. Wesley R. Burr, Reuben Hill, F. Ivan Nye, & Ira L. Reiss (eds.). New York: Free Press, pp. 549–581.

Gelles, R., & Straus, M. (1988). *Intimate violence*. New York: Simon & Schuster.

Hahn, D., Payne, W., & Lucas, E. (2011). *Focus on health* (10th ed). New York: McGraw-Hill.

Halpen, C. T., Oslak, S. G., Young, M. L., Martin, S. L., & Kukpper, L. L. (2001). Partner violence among adolescents in opposite-sex romantic relationships: Findings from the National Longitudinal Study of Adolescent Health. *American Journal of Public Health, 91*, 1679–1685.

Jasinski, J. L. (2004). Pregnancy and domestic violence: A review of the literature. *Trauma, Violence, and Abuse, 5*(1), 47–64.

National Center for Health Statistics (2008). *Health United States, 2007,* with Chartbook on Trends in the Health of Americans. Hyattsville, MD: Centers for Disease Control and Prevention.

Rouse, L. P. (1977). Domestic violence: Hitting us where we live. In *Analyzing social problems: Essays and exercises.* D. Dunn and D. V. Walker (eds.). Upper Saddle River, NJ: Prentice Hall, pp. 17–22.

Smith, P. H., White, J. W., & Holland, L. J. (2003). A longitudinal perspective on dating violence among adolescent and college-age women. *American Journal of Public Health, 93*(7), 1104–1109.

White, J. W., & Ross, M. P. (1991). Courtship violence: Incidence and prevalence in a national sample of higher education students. *Violence & Victimization, 6,* 247–256.

Zinn, B., Eitzen, S., & Wells, B. (2011). *Diversity in families.* Boston: Allyn & Bacon.

CHAPTER

5

Relationships

OBJECTIVES: STUDENTS WILL BE ABLE TO

1. Describe the factors that contribute to a healthy relationship.
2. Examine personal strategies for reducing tension in sexual communication.
3. Prepare a short list of why relationships fail.
4. Use several concepts in this chapter to construct a definition of love.
5. Apply critical thinking skill Level 3, Application.

HEALTHY RELATIONSHIPS

Perhaps the best thing a person could have is a wonderful relationship with someone. But how do you know if what you have is a healthy relationship? What qualities reflect a healthy relationship?

EFFECTIVE COMMUNICATION

Open communication involves active listening, attending (letting the person know you are listening without interrupting), and body language. Open communication involves minimizing distractions, including turning off your cell phone, radio, or TV.

When talking, be straightforward and say what you mean. The person to whom you are talking does not have ESP, so do not assume she/he can read your mind. Keep in mind that friends and partners do not always agree, so it is important to communicate the need to compromise as well.

ENHANCING INTIMATE COMMUNICATION: THREE RULES

1. When both partners have schedules that conflict on a regular basis, make a date. Mark a calendar indicating a regular weekly time for half an hour to discuss issues of importance.
2. Focus on the problem or behavior. Do not blame or attack the person by using phrases like "you always," or "if you hadn't done that." No one does *anything* all the time.
3. Take a break if needed. If the conversation is no longer effective, agree to continue discussing the matter at a later time. Don't just walk away and leave the other person hanging.

COMPROMISE

Mutual agreement should be the goal after the pros and cons about a certain situation are discussed. Keep in mind that concession works both ways. When both partners contribute to the solution to a problem, it becomes a win–win situation, not one in which one person is always conceding or getting the short end of the stick.

TRUST

A relationship built on mistrust is a relationship fraught with confusion, anger, and contempt. When one partner does not trust the other, neither person can grow in ways that are beneficial to each other. More time will be spent in arguing, looking over one's shoulder, or suspecting the worse to happen. More times than not, relationships that are not built on trust end in abject failure.

SEXUAL COMMUNICATION

Communicating about sexual issues can be most difficult. Most times, partners assume the sexual side of an intimate relationship will take care of itself. Sometimes couples assume that their partner should have *lover's intuition*, or know what the other likes and wants sexually.

Research indicates that good sexual communication enhances both overall satisfaction and sexual satisfaction in intimate relationships (Oattes & Offman 2007). In addition, effective sexual communication has been found to reduce unsafe sexual practices, increase sharing of information about sexually transmitted infections, and lead to more consistent use of contraception in teens and young adults (Farmer & Meston 2006; Quina et al. 2000). Two factors are crucial to effective sexual communication: sexual self-disclosure and learning how to communicate about sexual issues.

SEXUAL SELF-DISCLOSURE

According to Hock (2010), *sexual self-disclosure* is the process of revealing to your partner, in open and honest ways, any or all of the following:
- Sexual likes and dislikes, turn-ons and turn-offs
- Sexual needs and desires
- Sexual fears and concerns
- Questions about sexual transmitted diseases
- Past positive sexual experiences
- Personal sexual values and morals
- Personal conditions for a sexual relationship

Needless to say, sexual self-disclosure is not an easy task. It is highly likely that at the onset or during sexual communication, one or both partners may experience lack of information about human sexuality, embarrassment, or insecurity about using the right words such as vulva, penis, fellatio, cunnilingus, and other related terms. There is also the fear of rejection as a consequence of exposing too much information. However, love relationships that do not extend outside the proverbial comfort zone are unlikely to succeed anyway, so the benefits are usually worth the risks (Holt 2010).

STRATEGIES FOR IMPROVING SEXUAL COMMUNICATION

Learning to communicate sexually is a learned process. It requires time to get to know one another and, more importantly, time to know oneself. Here are suggestions for additional strategies for becoming more effective at sexual communication:
- Insist on your right to set a comfortable pace as the relationship progresses.
- Know what you want or don't want in a relationship *before* becoming sexually involved (Adapted from Michigan State University Counseling Center 2003).
- One way to get to know each other, particularly at the beginning of the relationship, is to talk about your parents' and grandparents' relationship. Learning about each other's *generation spirits*—attitudes, values, and behaviors passed down from past generations—could be very helpful in understanding behaviors. The old saying, "The apple doesn't fall too far from the tree," can enhance your understanding of your partner's sexual values, attitudes, and behaviors. Many times, this reduces the risk of relationship failure.

WHY RELATIONSHIPS FAIL

Relationships can be minefields, with several factors contributing to their failure. Here are a few.

LACK OF SELF-KNOWLEDGE

If you don't know yourself, how can you expect someone else to know you, let alone what you want? One should have knowledge about preferred lifestyle, favorite activities, morals, and values. Self-knowledge allows you to communicate who you are and what you want from your potential partner (Holt 2010).

IMBALANCES OF DECISION-MAKING POWER

When a relationship is marked by an imbalance in financial matters, choices of friends, everyday activities, and decision-making in general, it means that one partner has most of the power to make decisions that affect both partners (Blanc 2001). Let's be clear. A healthy power balance does not mean that every activity and decision must be equally balanced. What it does mean is that decisions are made by mutual agreement and neither partner feels unwillingly excluded from the decision-making process (Holt 2010).

ISOLATION

No two people can meet one another's needs all the time. When partners discourage outside connections, it may very well be a sign of fear and insecurity. Eventually, overdependence will stifle the relationship (Hock 2010).

LOW SELF-ESTEEM, INSECURITY, AND LACK OF SELF-CONFIDENCE

When people have low self-esteem, they usually feel unworthy of being loved and will look for their partners to validate proof of love, which can lead to dependence and possessiveness. The stronger partner may feel as if she/he is carrying the relationship while the weaker partner is not in a position to give much to the relationship. Unless lack of confidence is overcome, the relationship will fail (Hock 2010).

FAILING TO KEEP PROMISES, LYING, OR CHEATING

Betrayal of the basic trust necessary for a relationship to survive and thrive can unravel a relationship. Both partners must agree to abide by certain behaviors in order for the relationship to grow. But these agreements are only as good as the person's promise to carry through on them and her or his trust that the other person will do the same (Hock 2010).

REFLECTION

Because we are social beings, we have a basic need to love and to be loved. But how do we know how to love when there are few guidelines? The only guidelines we have are those that come from lived experiences, which requires taking risks. All relationships involve risk. By taking risks we grow, and if we are fortunate enough to choose a partner who truly loves us, she/he will grow as well.

CRITICAL THINKING SKILL

Level 3, Application. Solve problems to new situations by applying acquired knowledge, facts, techniques and rules in a different way.

Blooms Taxonomy Key Words. Prepare, demonstrate, examine, apply, interpret, modify, graph, and translate.

CRITICAL THINKING QUESTIONS FOR LEVEL 3, APPLICATION

1. Using key concepts learned in today's reading, modify the vignette located at the beginning of the chapter to fit your own experiences.
2. What facts can you use from today's readings to develop a definition of love?
3. What questions would you ask your partner in order to discover additional information as to her/his sexual values, beliefs, and behaviors?

WEBSITES

www.goaskalice.columbia.edu

The site features questions and answers of interest to young adults, including sexuality and sexual health.

www.siecus.org

Includes information updates and fact sheets on sexuality at different life stages, gay and lesbian issues, and approaches to sex education.

www.cyfc.umn.edu

The Children, Youth and Family Consortium offers research, programs, publications, and information on all types of parenting relationships, and family issues.

REFERENCES

Blanc, A. (2011). The effect of power in sexual relationships on sexual reproductive health: An examination of the evidence. *Studies in Family Planning, 32,* 189–213.

Farmer, M., & Meston, C. (2006). Predictors of condom use self-efficacy in an ethnically diverse university sample. *Archives of Sexual Behavior, 35,* 313–326.

Hock, R. R. (2010). *Human sexuality* (2nd ed). Upper Saddle River: Prentice Hall.

Oattes, M., Offman, A. (2007). Global self-esteem and sexual self-esteem as predictors of sexual communication in intimate relationships. *Canadian Journal of Human Sexuality, 16,* 89–100.

Quina, K., Harlow, L., Morokoff, P., Burkholder, G., & Deiter, P. (2000). Sexual communication in relationships. When words speak louder than actions. *Sex Roles, 42,* 523–549.

CHAPTER

6

Female Sexual Anatomy and Physiology

1. Understand the difference between primary and secondary sexual characteristics.
2. Identify the structures of the internal female sexual/reproductive anatomy.
3. Explain the female reproductive process.
4. Name the structures of the external female genitalia.
5. Distinguish between the cancers that can occur in the female reproductive system.
6. Apply critical thinking skill Level 1, Knowledge.

PRIMARY AND SECONDARY SEXUAL CHARACTERISTICS

Both females and males have primary and secondary sexual characteristics. The primary sexual characteristics present in the human body are directly involved in reproductive function. For example, ovaries in females and testes in males are needed for procreation. Secondary sexual characteristics are physical aspects typically associated with one sex but not the other (Jones & Lopez, 2006).

For example, as illustrated, women are more likely to have increased fat deposits around the hips, whereas men are more likely to have broader shoulders. In females, the vagina, cervix, uterus, and fallopian tubes all have a role to play in reproduction, and thus are considered primary sexual characteristics. Their specific functions are discussed next.

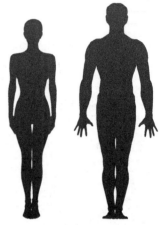

© 2011 by theromb. Used under license of Shutterstock, Inc.

INTERNAL FEMALE REPRODUCTIVE/SEXUAL ANATOMY

The internal reproductive anatomy consists of the vagina, cervix, uterus, fallopian tubes, and ovaries. The vagina and cervix are considered parts of the lower reproductive tract and the uterus, fallopian tubes, and ovaries are considered parts of the upper reproductive tract.

THE VAGINA

The vagina is a four-inch tube that functions as a passageway for the menstrual flow, as a receptacle for the penis during coitus (vaginal–penile intercourse), and as part of the birth canal (Jones and Lopez, 2006). The vagina is located behind the bladder and in front of the rectum. The vaginal walls are normally collapsed but can stretch during coitus and during a vaginal birth. The vagina has a balanced amount of "good" and "bad" bacteria to maintain an acidic environment that helps decrease microorganisms ascending into the upper reproductive tract (Ricci & Kyle, 2009). As you will read in subsequent chapters, this organ's strong defense system kills the majority of sperm. Vaginal discharge occurs throughout the menstrual cycle (regardless of sexual activity). This is normal and should be seen as the vagina getting rid of cellular debris. During menstruation and after (unprotected) coitus, the vaginal walls push any fluid out the introitus (vaginal opening).

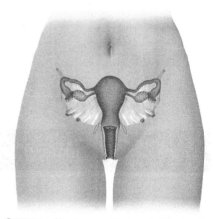

© 2011 by Alex Luengo. Used under license of Shutterstock, Inc.

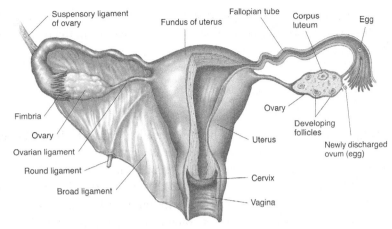

Suspensory ligament of ovary
Fundus of uterus
Fallopian tube
Corpus luteum
Egg
Fimbria
Ovary
Ovarian ligament
Round ligament
Broad ligament
Ovary
Uterus
Developing follicles
Newly discharged ovum (egg)
Cervix
Vagina

Copyright © Kendall Hunt Publishing Company.

Many women are advised by well-meaning relatives and friends to douche to get rid of unwanted odor or fluid from the vagina. But vaginal cleansing, such as douching, harms the pH balance that could predispose women to vaginal infections like bacterial vaginosis (discussed in Chapter 10). The vagina needs to be seen as a "self-cleaning oven"—leave it alone and let it do its job! Any abnormal discharge that isn't consistent with a woman's normal secretions should be seen by a doctor instead of trying to self-medicate with over-the-counter feminine hygiene products.

Glands near the vaginal opening secrete mucus to keep the vaginal lining moist. The vaginal lining can tear if the vagina is not properly lubricated during coitus. This can increase the risk of infection, so care should be taken before penetration to ensure the vaginal lining will not be injured. Water-based lubricants that may be used to facilitate penile penetration will not harm the vaginal lining and can be used frequently. If penetration is painful, regardless of adequate lubrication, then such activity should cease until the cause is found and rectified. Keep in mind that there are numerous sensual activities possible that are pleasurable for both partners and do not require penetration.

THE CERVIX

The cervix is considered to be the lower part of the uterus (*cervix* means neck in Latin). The cervix connects the body of the uterus to the vagina. The endocervix is the part of the cervix closest to the uterus. The part next to the vagina is called the ectocervix. The ectocervix has a small opening called the os. The shedding of the endometrial lining emerges from the os to the vagina. The cervix contains glands that secrete mucus (that is acidic) to plug the cervix (and the os) to prevent sperm or other microorganisms from entering the uterus (Jones & Lopez, 2006).

When ovulation (a mature ovarian follicle containing an oocyte is released from an ovary) occurs, the cervix produces mucus that is hospitable to sperm, allowing any live sperm (that have survived the vagina!) to travel through it to enter the uterus to make their way to the fallopian tubes to find the ovum (or egg) to fertilize (Ricci & Kyle, 2009).

As soon as a pregnancy is established, the cervix creates a special antibacterial mucosal plug to block passage of microorganisms to the upper reproductive tract (Jones & Lopez, 2006). This helps reduce the risk of

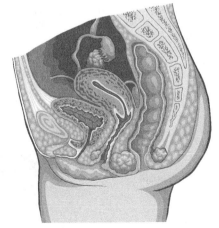

© 2011 by Alex Luengo. Used under license of Shutterstock, Inc.

infection ascending into the uterus and harming the fetus. The cervix plays a vital role during the first stage of labor, as well. Contractions are focused on thinning out and dilating the cervix to 10 centimeters (which is around

4 inches) in order to allow the fetus to go through the vaginal canal to be pushed out by the mother. If a vaginal birth has not occurred, then the os has an oval opening. After a vaginal birth, the os is converted into a transverse slit (Ricci & Kyle, 2009).

THE UTERUS

The uterus is an inverted pear-shaped organ that is held in place by ligaments that can stretch (as can the uterus) when a woman is pregnant (Jones & Lopez, 2006). The uterus is located in front of the rectum and behind the bladder. The body of the uterus is called the corpus. When a female is not pregnant, the uterus is the size of her fist.

The uterus has three layers of tissue (Ricci & Kyle, 2009). The external surface of the uterus is called the perimetrium. Inside the perimetrium is a thick layer of smooth muscle called the myometrium. The strong uterine contractions that a pregnant woman feels during labor come from the myometrium. The layer of the uterus that lines the uterine cavity is called the endometrium. This is the layer that is shed during menstruation and the layer in which the blastocyst (discussed in Chapter 9) implants itself to become a pregnancy (Jones & Lopez, 2006). Unlike the other layers, the endometrium is under the control of progesterone, and it endures distinct transformation in structure and function throughout the menstrual cycle. The endometrial lining is at its thinnest just after menstruation and it is at its thickest during the part of the menstrual cycle in which the blastocyst would be expected to enter the uterus (Ricci & Kyle, 2009).

A woman's menstrual cycle averages 28 days, but can range from 21 to 35 days and can vary every month. A woman will experience uterine bleeding for an average of 4 days, but that can vary from 2 to 6 days (Nelson & Baldwin, 2007). In the United States, the monthly flow of blood and cellular debris (called menses) usually starts around the age of 12½. Women experience menopause (discussed later in this chapter) around the age of 51 (Alexander et al., 2007). During this timeframe, women will bleed around 13 times a year for almost 40 years. Given such statistics, more women should seriously consider buying feminine hygiene products in bulk!

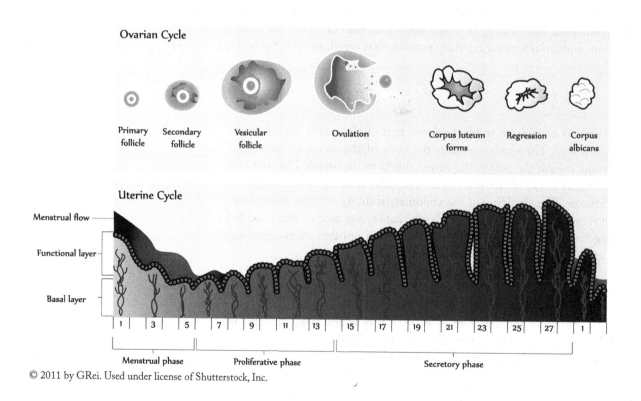

© 2011 by GRei. Used under license of Shutterstock, Inc.

THE FALLOPIAN TUBES

The fallopian tubes, named after the sixteenth-century anatomist Fallopius, are about 4 inches in length and have a diameter about the size of a drinking straw, or around ½ an inch (Jones & Lopez 2006). The fallopian tubes are lined with cilia (hair-like extensions on cells) that beat toward the uterus. When ovulation occurs, the ovum is captured by the ends of the fallopian tube called the fimbriae.

Fertilization (union of one egg and one sperm) must take place near the end of the fallopian tube in order to increase the chances of a successful implantation in the uterus in about a week's time. Unfortunately, the fallopian tubes can be harmed by bacterial infections such as chlamydia and gonorrhea (which are sexually transmitted) and bacterial vaginosis (which is not sexually transmitted). The irreplicable damage to the fallopian tubes caused by any of these reproductive tract infections can lead to an ectopic pregnancy (a life-threatening condition that requires immediate medical attention). These reproductive tract infections are discussed in Chapter 10.

THE OVARY

The ovaries are almond-shaped organs that are connected to the uterus and pelvic wall by supportive ligaments. They serve two functions in female reproduction: the development and maturation of oocytes (or eggs) and the production of three hormones (Jones & Lopez, 2006). These hormones are estrogen, progesterone, and testosterone.

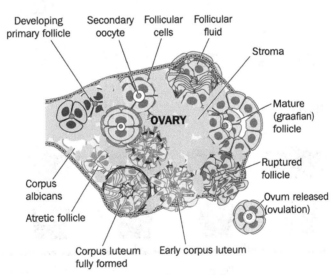

© 2011 by Blamb. Used under license of Shutterstock, Inc.

Females are born with all their eggs. According to the American Congress of Obstetricians and Gynecologists (ACOG), by the fifth month of pregnancy, the eggs have formed in the ovaries of a female fetus (ACOG, 2010). At birth, a female infant is born with about 5 million immature ovarian follicles, which decrease to about 500,000 by puberty (Speroff & Fritz, 2005). That number continues to decline as females get older. By the age of 35, there will be fewer than 100,000, and by menopause the follicular supply will be nearly depleted (Jones & Lopez, 2006).

Most women will ovulate one ovum (ova is plural) once a month over a 40-year reproductive lifespan. That means women will ovulate around 400 to 500 times during their fertile years. An ovum is viable for fertilization for around 24 to 48 hours (Ricci & Kyle, 2009). Most of these ova are not fertilized, and women will menstruate anywhere from 14 to 20 days *after* ovulation occurs (Ricci & Kyle, 2009).

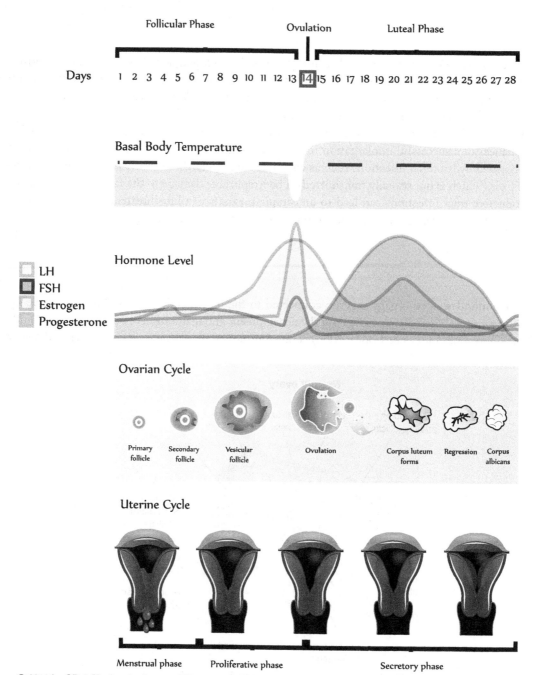

Follicular Phase | Ovulation | Luteal Phase

Days   1 2 3 4 5 6 7 8 9 10 11 12 13 **14** 15 16 17 18 19 20 21 22 23 24 25 26 27 28

Basal Body Temperature

Hormone Level

☐ LH
◼ FSH
☐ Estrogen
▨ Progesterone

Ovarian Cycle

Primary follicle | Secondary follicle | Vesicular follicle | Ovulation | Corpus luteum forms | Regression | Corpus albicans

Uterine Cycle

Menstrual phase | Proliferative phase | Secretory phase

© 2011 by GRei. Used under license of Shutterstock, Inc.

Women's fertile years in the United States have changed dramatically relative to our hunter-gatherer ancestors (Jones & Lopez, 2006). For example, thousands of years ago, females experienced menarche around the age of 16. Girls now start menstruating 3½ years earlier. We used to give birth to our first child around the age of 19. Now we give birth for the first time around the age of 25 (the oldest average age for a first birth on record for this country). An average completed family size used to include 5 children. Now, on average, women have around 2 children in their lifetime. Thousands of years ago, women breastfed their baby for 3 years. Today, women breastfeed their baby for 3 months (CDC, 2007).

Why are females menstruating earlier, starting a family later in life, having a smaller family size and breastfeeding for a considerably less time period? We can attribute the "birth" of modern industrialized societies to the changes in fertility. Like many societies similar to ours, the United States has changed significantly by the advances of agricultural, industrial, and medical industries (Jones & Lopez, 2006). That is not to say these advances have not been beneficial to society. Our life expectancy has increased and our maternal/infant mortality has decreased, and these industries can take much of the credit for this.

FEMALE REPRODUCTIVE PROCESS

Cholesterol is needed for the development and secretion of the hormones by the ovaries (Jones & Lopez, 2006). Cholesterol is made by the liver. We don't need any extra from the food we eat because our bodies make all that we need. As previously mentioned, these hormones are estrogen, progesterone, and testosterone. Testosterone is also made by the female's adrenal glands. The secretion of these hormones and the maturation of the ovarian follicles are controlled by the release of follicle-stimulating hormone (FSH) and luteinizing hormone (LH) in the pituitary gland (Jones & Lopez, 2006). Figure 6.1 illustrates how these two hormones orchestrate the menstrual cycle.

At puberty, estrogen helps in the development of secondary sexual characteristics. As previously mentioned, secondary sexual characteristics are features that distinguish females and male, but are not attributes that are directly part of the reproductive system. For example, in females, the development of breasts is considered a secondary sexual characteristic. Even though many countries (but not all) around the world have placed a sexual meaning to female breasts, they are not considered part of the reproductive process because they are not needed for procreation to occur.

Female breasts, though, can provide optimal nutrients to a newborn and infant. The American Academy of Pediatrics Work Group on Breastfeeding (2005) recommends exclusive breastfeeding for the first six months of life. Breastfeeding is associated with decreased infant risk for many early-life diseases and conditions, as well as health

FIGURE 6.1: The Menstrual Cycle

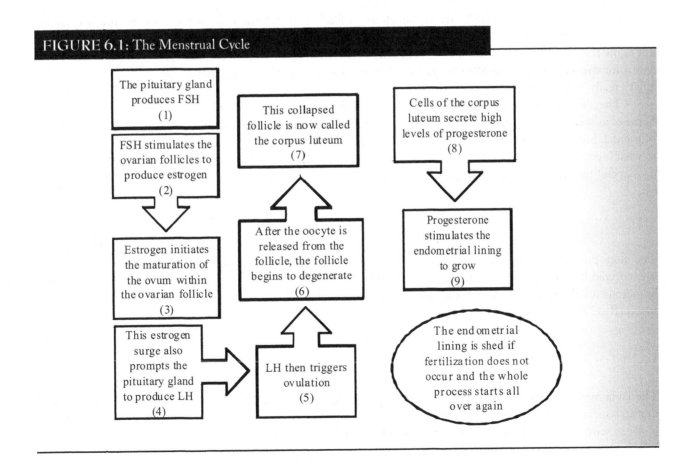

benefits to the mother, including decreased risk for type-2 diabetes, ovarian cancer, and breast cancer (Ip et al., 2007). Moreover, producing more milk requires additional energy and should lead to greater postpartum weight loss (Baker et al., 2008). Also, lactation improves glucose tolerance in the early postpartum period and longer duration of breastfeeding has been associated with lower maternal weight gain 10 to 15 years later (Gunderson et al, 2007).

MENOPAUSE

According to the North American Menopause Society, menopause is considered the permanent end of menstruation and fertility. All women will eventually experience menopause. It is a normal, natural event when the ovaries will cease producing estrogen, progesterone, and testosterone and will no longer release an ovum from an ovary (Nelson & Stewart, 2007). As previously mentioned, women in the Unites States go through menopause around the age of 51 (Alexander et al., 2007). One percent of women are menopausal before the age of 40 and around 2 percent of women have not experienced menopause by the age of 55. Half of all women will not experience any symptoms associated with menopause, such as hot flashes (the scientific name is vasomotor symptoms), night sweats, sleep disturbances, and irritability (Jones & Lopez, 2006). Research has found that women who are overweight or obese, smoke, and who are stressed out are more likely to experience hot flashes. Months or years leading up to menopause, women can experience many of the symptoms listed, as well as menstruating erratically. This is known as perimenopause.

EXTERNAL FEMALE GENITALIA

Girls and women in the United States are much more likely to recall the clinical terms to the internal female reproductive anatomy than a female's external genitals. Even though many of us do not know the clinical terms to this area of the body, we were raised with very colorful words for the female genitalia. Why do you think that's the case? Let's take a look at what's really "down there."

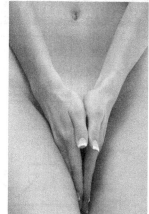

The *vulva* is the clinical term that covers all of the female external genitals. Some of us were raised calling this area the *vagina*, but that part of the female anatomy is internal, not external. The vulva varies greatly in appearance. There is no set standard to what is considered "normal." Moreover, sexual pleasure is not determined by the size or shape of the vulva. The vulva includes the following.

© 2011 by carlo dapino. Used under license of Shutterstock, Inc.

MONS PUBIS

The mons pubis, which has also been called the mons veneris, is a cushion of fatty tissue, covered by skin and pubic hair forming an inverted pyramid. This area contains numerous touch receptors, which means the mons pubis can be very sensitive to the touch (Ricci & Kyle, 2009).

LABIA MAJORA

The labia majora are fleshy folds of tissue that extend down from the mons pubis and surround the vaginal and urethral openings. This area contains fat, sweat and oil glands, as well as pubic hair on the pigmented skin. This area is not as sensitive to the touch as the mons pubis (Jones & Lopez, 2006).

LABIA MINORA

The labia minora are paired folds of smooth tissue underlying the labia majora. They are fleshy-looking in color and are hairless, but contain oil glands. They are abundant with nerve endings, thus making this area highly sensitive. They swell when a woman becomes sexually aroused (Ricci & Kyle, 2008). They vary in size and have become a focal point in women who feel their genitals are "abnormal looking." Unfortunately, women with this negative attitude can opt to have their labia minora surgically altered, a practice called labiaplasty. This relatively new cosmetic surgical procedure is known to decrease vulvar sensitivity.

GLANS OF THE CLITORIS

Most people believe that the external part of the clitoris is the only part of the clitoris. The whole clitoris is found both internally and externally, encompass thousands of nerve endings and contain erectile tissue (spongy tissue with blood vessels that engorge with blood to cause an erection). The external part is located above the urethral opening. It increases in size when a woman becomes sexually aroused. This is the only organ in the human body that's sole purpose is sexual pleasure (Katz, 2007). There is no part of the male body that its sole purpose is sexual pleasure. Touching the glans of the clitoris can be very uncomfortable, if not painful to the touch. When this area is stimulated effectively, though, a woman can experience an array of pleasurable sensations.

CLITORAL HOOD

The clitoral hood is a fold of skin that covers and protects the glans of the clitoris (Jones & Lopez, 2006). During sexual arousal, as the glans of the clitoris engorge with blood, it "hides" behind the clitoral hood.

URETHRAL OPENING

The vulva has three openings that can lead to outside the body. The urethral opening allows liquid waste to leave a female's body. The Skene's glands are located on either side of the urethral opening. These glands secrete mucus to keep the urethral opening moist and lubricated for the passage of urine (Schuiling & Likis, 2006). The Skene's glands are also believed to ejaculate a fluid in some women (it is unknown why some women ejaculate and why some women don't) during orgasm. This fluid does not contain urine and is similar to the fluid developed by a male's prostate gland (discussed in Chapter 7). The Skene's glands are homologous to the prostate gland. The Skene's glands have been referred to as the "female prostate." But it is an error to identify these glands as such, because both the Skene's and prostate glands were developed from the same embryonic tissue. They were provided different names because their function is not exactly the same and their physical structure does not carry much resemblance.

INTROITUS

The opening to the vagina is called the introitus. This is the opening that menstrual blood will flow out of, a baby can be born from, and an erect penis can enter. If a woman is sexually aroused, through tiny ducts beside the lower portion of the introitus, the Bartholin's glands secrete mucus that provides vaginal lubrication (Schuiling & Likis, 2006).

The hymen is a fold of mucous membrane that surrounds or partially covers the introitus at birth. Its purpose is unknown, even though many cultures throughout history have used the (perceived) absence of the hymen as indication that a woman has participated in coitus. Any tearing of the hymen is not an indication that a female has had a penis in her vagina, though (Mattson & Smith, 2004). The hymen can tear by participating in numerous physical activities, such as certain sports, like horseback riding. The hymen remains intact, though stretched, after penile penetration. The hymen is not completely removed until a vaginal birth has occurred.

PERINEUM

The area of the perineum is located between the introitus and the anus. It contains numerous nerve endings that indicate that it is sensitive to the touch (Ricci & Kyle, 2009). A surgical incision to this area can be performed if a pregnant woman is having difficulty pushing the baby out. This procedure is called an episiotomy. Males also have a perineum, and it's called a perineum!

ANUS

The anus is the external opening of the rectum. There is no difference between a female and a male's anus. This area allows solid waste to be expelled from the body. The area has a relatively high concentration of nerve endings that suggest sensitivity to the touch. The anus does not contain glands to moisten the area so a water-based lubricant is required if penetration is expected.

CANCER OF THE FEMALE REPRODUCTIVE SYSTEM

When women think about cancer, many think of breast cancer and/or cervical cancer (depending on age and media exposure). One in eight women will be diagnosed with breast cancer, and most of them will be over the age of 60. Breast cancer is discussed in Chapter 13. Along with cervical cancer, cancer of the vulva, vagina, uterus, and ovaries are also possible. Each of these cancers is discussed in this section. Three out of the five cancers discussed in this chapter are primarily caused by human papillomavirus or HPV, a sexually transmitted infection (zur Hausen, 2009).

CANCER STATISTICS

The American Cancer Society's most recent estimates for cancers of the female reproductive organs in the United States are for 2010 (American Cancer Society, 2010). In that year, 83,750 women were diagnosed with a cancer of one of five reproductive organs: cervical, ovarian, uterine, vaginal, or vulvar. Almost half of all cancers of the female reproductive organs were reported developing in the uterus. About 43,470 cases of uterine cancer (which includes cancer of the body of the uterus and the endometrial lining) were diagnosed, and around 7,950 women died from it. About 21,880 women were diagnosed with ovarian cancer and around 13,850 women died from it. For invasive cervical cancer, about 12,200 were diagnosed and about 4,210 women died from it. About 3,900 vulvar cancers were diagnosed and around 920 women died from it. Vaginal cancer is rare—about 2,300 new cases were diagnosed and about 780 women died from it (American Cancer Society, 2010).

CANCER OF THE CERVIX

Around 15 percent of all cancers of the female reproductive organs are cervical cancer (American Cancer Society, 2010). Given the media exposure of preventing cervical cancer, most women believe they are at a higher risk of cervical cancer than uterine cancer. As the statistics above show, that is not the case, though (at least not in the United States). Cancer of the cervix is the second most common cancer in women worldwide (what do you think is the first?), with about 500,000 new cases and 250,000 deaths each year (zur Hausen, 2009).

In the United States, 1 in 40 women will be diagnosed with uterine cancer, but 1 in 156 women will be diagnosed with cervical cancer. Surprised? Why do you think there is so much more media hype to cervical cancer than endometrial cancer? Partly, this is due to prevention. Unlike most cases of uterine cancer, cervical cancer is preventable.

Primary Prevention   Primary prevention of cervical cancer means a woman does not place herself at risk of factors that are known to cause this cancer. Ninety percent of cervical cancers are believed to be caused by HPV (American Cancer Society, 2010). As previously mentioned, HPV is a sexually transmitted infection (STI) that can be passed on by participating in (unprotected) coitus, anal intercourse, oral sex and skin-to-skin contact by an infected partner.

Abstinence is the best way to prevent exposure. Because the majority of us will (eventually) participate in sexual activity with another person, abstinence will not always be a realistic option. Thus, condom use must be used consistently with every type of sexual act to prevent fluid transmission and skin-to-skin contact to *reduce* risk. According to the Centers for Disease Control and Prevention, condoms may also lower the risk of developing HPV-related diseases, such as genital warts and cervical cancer. But HPV can infect areas that are not covered by a condom, such as the labia majora and labia minora in females, the scrotum in males and the perineum and buttocks in both sexes, so condoms may not *fully* protect against HPV (CDC, 2009). Unless it is known that each person is not infected with HPV (or any other STI), precautions must always been taken. Keep in mind that no observable symptoms is *never* an indication that an individual is not infected, especially with HPV and especially with the HPV types that increase one's risk to cancer. Also, the more sexual partners a person has, the more likely one will be exposed to HPV.

Unlike other viral STIs (like genital herpes and HIV), a vaccine has been developed that can protect both women and men from some strains of HPV infection. This is discussed in detail in Chapter 10.

The other 10 percent of cervical cancers are believed to be caused by smoking. According to the American Cancer Society (2010), women who smoke are twice as likely as nonsmokers to develop cervical cancer. Smoking carries many cancer-causing substances that affect organs all over the body. Interestingly, tobacco byproducts have been found in the cervical mucus of women who smoke. Researchers believe that these harmful chemicals damage the DNA of cervical cells and may contribute to the development of cervical cancer. Never picking up a cigarette or cigar can help prevent cervical cancer caused by this addictive behavior.

According to the American Cancer Society (2010), there are other factors that may influence (but are not known to cause) abnormal changes in the cervical cells due to HPV or smoking. One factor is having a family history of cervical cancer. This may mean that a woman inherited defective genes that do not help the body fight off abnormal cervical changes. Having a compromised immune system is another factor. This can happen if a woman is HIV+ or has already been diagnosed with another cancer. Both of these medical conditions can slow a body's ability to find off abnormal cervical changes. Having had three or more full-term pregnancies is also a factor, but it is unknown why this is the case. Giving birth before the age of 17 is another factor that may increase a woman's risk to cervical cancer. This may be partly due to participating in sexual activities at an early age, which could lead to more sexual partners in one's lifetime and increased likelihood of being exposed to HPV. Also, a young woman's cervix is more susceptible to infection, which could lead to the growth of abnormal cervical cells.

Using oral contraceptives for more than five years is also believed to be a factor. This is partly due to the decreased use of condoms during this time period, but hormonal methods may also change the ability of the cervical cells to fight off abnormal cervical changes. Living in poverty can also increase a woman's chances of developing cervical cancer later in life. This is partly due to lack of access to medical care that could help prevent abnormal cervical cell growth from developing into cervical cancer (American Cancer Society, 2010).

Secondary Prevention   Secondary prevention of cervical cancer means a woman is screened to attempt to diagnose and treat abnormal cervical cells in its early stages before it progresses to cervical dysplasia (precancerous cells) and cancer. The rate of cervical cancer has been declining in this country since the 1940s, when Dr. George Papanicolaou invented the Papanicolaou test (also called the Pap smear) to detect abnormal cells on the cervix (Winer & Koutsky, 2008).

A Pap smear is performed when a doctor removes a sample of cells and mucus by gently scraping the ectocervix (part of the cervix closest to the vagina) with a special instrument. The ACOG (2009) recommends all women to begin receiving a Pap smear (every three years) starting at the age of 21 (regardless of sexual activity with men). From that invention, doctors were able to discover which women were at risk of cervical cancer and developed methods to stop the spread and/or formation of cancerous cells.

Between 1955 and 1992, the death rate from cervical cancer declined by almost 80 percent (Balasubramanian, Palefsky & Koutsky, 2008)! At one time, over 35,000 women *a year* were diagnosed with cervical cancer in this country. If abnormal cervical cells are detected, newer tests look for the genes identifying the presence of HPV in the cervical cells (Cox, 2006). This test is called the HPV DNA test. Because most women who develop cervical cancer will not do so until after the age of 30, the HPV DNA test is recommended for women only over the age of 30. Any woman, regardless of age, can ask her medical provider if this test is right for her.

The cervix is covered by two main types of cells. The ectocervix is covered by squamous cells and the endocervix is covered by glandular cells. Both of these cells meet in an area called the transformation zone. According to the American Cancer Society (2010), most cervical cancers begin in the transformation zone. About 80 to 90 percent of cervical cancers are squamous cell carcinomas. These cancers are from the squamous cells that cover the surface of the ectocervix. About two-thirds of all cervical cancers are caused by HPV 16 and 18 (zur Hausen, 2009).

In the United Sates, most cervical cancers are diagnosed in women under the age of 50. Around 20 percent are found in women over the age of 65. Cervical cancer rarely develops in women under the age of 20. African American women develop cervical cancer about 50 percent more often than non-Hispanic white women. Hispanic women are twice as likely as non-Hispanic white women to be diagnosed with cervical cancer (American Cancer Society, 2010).

Tertiary Prevention   Tertiary prevention of cervical cancer aims to reduce the negative impact of this established disease by restoring function and reducing disease-related complications. If a woman is suspected of having precancerous or cancer cells on her cervix, she will have her cervix biopsied. What this means is that tissue from either the ectocervix or endocervix (or both) will be removed for further testing. Some women may have a cone biopsy done, in which a cone-shaped piece of tissue is removed from the cervix for further analysis and to remove suspicious cervical cells. Cells from the ectocervix, endocervix, and in the transformation zone are contained within the tissue.

Abnormal cells can be destroyed with cryosurgery or laser surgery. With cryosurgery, liquid nitrogen is used to kill the abnormal cells on the cervix by freezing them. With laser surgery, a focused beam of high-energy light is used to burn off the abnormal tissue

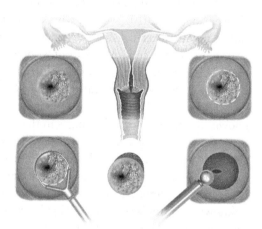

© 2011 by Alex Luengo. Used under license of Shutterstock, Inc.

from the cervix. Depending on the severity of the damage to the cervix and the chances of a full recovery, future pregnancies may not be able to be carried to term.

CANCER OF THE VULVA

Vulvar cancer accounts for about 4 percent of cancers of the female reproductive organs in the United States (American Cancer Society, 2010), 80 percent of which are caused by HPV (zur Hausen, 2009). Even though the vulva consists of many structures of the external female genitals, this cancer usually implies that the labia majora, labia minora or glans of the clitoris has been invaded by cancerous cells. The labia majora is the most common site and accounts for about 50 percent of cases, with the labia minora coming in second with 15 to 20 percent of cases (Winer & Koutsky, 2008).

CANCER OF THE VAGINA

About 1 percent of cancers of the female reproductive system are vaginal cancers (American Cancer Society, 2010). The vagina is lined by a layer of flat cells called squamous cells. Seventy percent of vaginal cancers begin in the squamous cells. These cancers are more common in the upper area of the vagina near the cervix. Fifteen percent of vaginal cancer begin in the gland cells of the vagina (this is called adenocarcinoma) and are found near the vaginal opening. This cancer typically develops in women older than 50.

Even though most of us think of skin cancer when we hear the term *melanoma* (discussed in Chapter 13), 9 percent of vaginal cancers that occur in the lower portion of the vagina are believed to be melanoma. Up to 4 percent of vaginal cancers are sarcomas. A sarcoma is a cancer that begins in the cells of bones, muscles, or connective tissue. These cancers form deep in the wall of the vagina, not on its surface (American Cancer Society, 2010).

According to the American Cancer Society (2010), up to 90 percent of vaginal cancers are caused by HPV. Almost half of the cases occur in women who are 70 years old or older. Only 15 percent of cases are found in women younger than 40. Similar to cervical cancer, the other 10 percent is thought to be caused by smoking. Most vaginal cancers do not cause symptoms until after they have reached an advanced stage. A Pap smear test can help detect any abnormal cells in the cervix that could have ascended from the vagina. More testing will be performed to locate what areas are cancerous and need to be treated.

Other factors that may influence (but are not known to cause) abnormal changes in the vaginal cells due to HPV or smoking are having personally experienced cervical cancer, having a compromised immune system, and having a family history of vaginal cancer. Studies have shown that there is an abnormality of chromosome 3 in many vaginal cancers, which could indicate an inherited genetic defect that can increase a woman's risk to cancer of the vagina (American Cancer Society, 2010).

CANCER OF THE UTERUS

According to the American Cancer Society (2010), cancer of the endometrium is the most common cancer (around 50 percent) of the female reproductive organs in the United States. Why is that the case? After the person becomes an adult, most cells in the body divide only to replace worn-out or dying cells or to repair injuries, but the cells of the inner lining of the uterus, the endometrium, divide based on a woman's monthly menstrual cycle. Constant cell division can increase the risk of one cell not dividing properly or dying off when it is expected to. Moreover, the endometrium is influenced by the hormone estrogen, which is supplied by the ovaries. As previously mentioned, the ovaries also produce progesterone, but a shift in the balance of these two hormones toward more estrogen increases a woman's risk for developing endometrial cancer. Endometrial cancer is rare in women under the age of 40. Most cases are found in women 50 years and older (American Cancer Society, 2010).

Depending on the stage of the cancer, a hysterectomy may have to be performed to reduce the risk of the cancer spreading to the lymph nodes or other parts of the body. A hysterectomy is the surgical removal of the uterus. If the cancer has spread to other reproductive organs, a radical hysterectomy removes the ovaries, fallopian tubes, uterus, cervix, and upper portion of the vagina.

CANCER OF THE OVARIES

Ovarian cancer accounts for about 3 percent of all cancers in women, but around 25 percent of all cancers of the female reproductive organs. According to the American Cancer Society (2010), ovarian cancer is the ninth most common cancer among women, excluding non-melanoma skin cancers. It ranks fifth in cancer deaths among women, accounting for more deaths than any other cancer of the female reproductive system. This cancer mainly develops in older women (American Cancer Society, 2010). Ovarian cancer is rare in women younger than 40. About half of the women who are diagnosed with ovarian cancer are 60 years or older. Women who are considered obese (women with a body mass index of at least 30) have a higher risk of developing this cancer. Women with a family history of breast and ovarian cancer also have a higher risk of developing this cancer. If necessary, the ovary or ovaries can be surgically removed to decrease the chance of the cancer spreading to the lymph nodes or other parts of the body. This procedure is called an oophorectomy.

REFLECTIONS

The purpose of this chapter was to familiarize students with the female sexual and reproductive anatomy and the cancers that can occur to the female reproductive system. Gaining knowledge and understanding of our bodies can be an important aspect of women's and men's sexual well-being and sexual intelligence. Many women are unacquainted with their genitals and/or their internal reproductive structures. Why do you think there may be individuals in your class that do not know some of the terms for the female sexual/reproductive anatomy? When do you think this information should be taught, and by whom? Do you think men should be informed as well as women on the female sexual/reproductive anatomy?

CRITICAL THINKING SKILL

Level 1, Knowledge. Exhibit memory of previously learned material by recalling facts, terms, basic concepts, and answers.

Bloom's Taxonomy Key Words. Count, define, list, match, name, outline, recall, state, write, identify.

CRITICAL THINKING QUESTIONS

1. How can women decrease their risk to cancer in their reproductive organs?
2. Genital piercing and cosmetic labiaplasty are becoming more common in the Western world. How are these procedures similar to and different from the genital cutting done to women and girls in parts of Africa, the Middle East, and Asia?
3. What messages about menstruation do you observe in advertising and television programs?

WEBSITES

www.cancer.org

The American Cancer Society has many resources regarding cancer.

www.menopause.org

The North American Menopause Society is dedicated to promoting the health and quality of life of women entering menopause and beyond.

http://www.ourbodiesourselves.org/

Our Bodies Ourselves is a comprehensive website offering information on women's health issues.

REFERENCES

Alexander, L., LaRosa, J., Bader, H., & Garfield, S. (2007). *New dimensions in women's health* (3rd ed.). Sudbury, MA: Jones & Bartlett Publishers.

American Academy of Pediatrics Work Group on Breastfeeding. (2005). Breastfeeding and the use of human milk. *Pediatrics, 115,* 496–506.

American Cancer Society (2010). *Cancer facts and figures 2010.* Atlanta, GA: American Cancer Society.

American Congress of Obstetricians and Gynecologists (2009). ACOG Practice Bulletin no. 109: Cervical Cytology Screening. *Obstetrics & Gynecology, 114,* 1409–1420.

American Congress of Obstetricians and Gynecologists (2010). *How your baby grows during pregnancy.* Danvers, MA: The American College of Obstetricians and Gynecologists.

Baker, J., Gamborg, M., Heitmann, B., Lissner, L., Sorensen, T., & Rasmussen, K. (2008). Breastfeeding reduces postpartum weight retention. *American Journal of Clinical Nutrition, 88*(6), 1543–1551.

Balasubramanian, A., Palefsky, J., & Koutsky, L. (2008). Cervical neoplasia and other STD-related genital tract neoplasias. In K. Holmes, P. Sparling, W. Stamm, P. Piot, J. Wasserheit, L. Corey, & M. Cohen (eds.), *Sexually Transmitted Diseases* (4th ed.), pp. 1051–1074. New York, NY: McGraw-Hill.

Cartwright, R., & Cardozo, L. (2008). Cosmetic vulvovaginal surgery. *Obstetrics, Gynecology & Reproductive Medicine, 18*(10), 285–286.

Centers for Disease Control and Prevention (CDC) (2007). Breastfeeding trends and updated national health objectives for exclusive breastfeeding—United States, birth years 2000–2004. *Morbidity & Mortality Weekly Report, 56,* 760–763.

Centers for Disease Control and Prevention (CDC) (2009). Genital HPV infection—Fact sheet. *Sexually Transmitted Diseases,* www.cdc.gov/std/HPV/STDFact-HPV.htm.

Cox, J. (2006). Human papillomavirus testing in primary cervical screening and abnormal Papanicolaou management. *Obstetrical & Gynecological Survey, 61,* (Supplemental 1), S15–S25.

Gunderson, E., Lewis, C., Tsai, A., Chiang, V., Carnethon, M., Quesenberry, C., & Sidney, S. (2007). A 20-year prospective study of childbearing and incidence of diabetes in young women, controlling for glycemia before conception: The coronary artery risk development in young adults (CARDIA) study. *Diabetes, 56,* 2990–2996.

Ip, S., Chung, M., Raman, G., et al. (2007). *Breastfeeding and maternal and infant health outcomes in developed countries.* Rockville, MD: United States Department of Health & Human Services.

Jones, R. & Lopez, K. (2006). *Human Reproductive Biology,* 3rd ed. Burlington, MA: Elsevier.

Katz, A. (2007). Sexuality and women. *Nursing for Women's Health, 11*(1), 37–43.

Mattson, S., & Smith, J. (2004). *Core curriculum for maternal newborn nursing* (3rd ed.). St. Louis, MO: Elsevier Saunders.

Nelson, A., & Baldwin, S. (2007). Menstrual disorders and related concerns. In R. Hatcher, J. Trussell, A. Nelson, W. Cates, F. Stewart, & D. Kowal (eds.), *Contraceptive Technology,* 19th ed., pp. 451–498. New York, NY: Ardent Media.

Nelson, A., & Stewart F. (2007). Menopause and perimenopausal health. In R. Hatcher, J. Trussell, A. Nelson, W. Cates, F. Stewart, & D. Kowal (eds.), *Contraceptive Technology,* 19th ed., pp. 699–746. New York, NY: Ardent Media.

Paarlberg, K., & Weijenborg, P. (2008). Request for operative reduction of the labia minora; a proposal for a practical guideline for gynecologists. *Journal of Psychosomatic Obstetrics & Gynecology, 29*(4), 230–234.

Ricci, S., & Kyle, T. (2009). *Maternity and pediatric nursing.* Philadelphia, PA: Lippincott Williams & Wilkins.

Schuiling, K., & Likis, F. (2006). *Women's gynecologic health*. Sudbury, MA: Jones & Barlett Publishers.

Smith Oboler, R. (2001). Law and persuasion in the elimination of female genital modification. *Society for Applied Anthropology, 60*(4), 311–318.

Speroff, L., & Fritz, M. (2005). *Clinical gynecologic endocrinology & infertility* (7th ed.). Philadelphia, PA: Lippincott Williams & Wilkins.

Talle, A. (2001). Female genital mutilation. In N. Smelser & P. Baltes (eds.), *International Encyclopedia of the Social & Behavioral Sciences*, pp. 5447–5451. Oxford, United Kingdom: Elsevier Science Ltd.

Winer, R., & Koutsky, L. (2008). Genital human papillomavirus infection (2008). In K. Holmes, P. Sparling, W. Stamm, P. Piot, J. Wasserheit, L. Corey, & M. Cohen (eds.), *Sexually Transmitted Diseases*, 4th ed., pp. 489–508. New York, NY: McGraw-Hill.

zur Hausen, H. (2009). Papillomaviruses in the causation of human cancers—A brief historical account. *Virology, 384*, 260–265.

CHAPTER

7

Male Sexual Anatomy and Physiology

1. Understand the difference between primary and secondary sexual characteristics.
2. Name the structures of the external male genitalia.
3. Identify the structures of the internal male sexual/reproductive anatomy.
4. Explain the male reproductive process.
5. Define erectile dysfunction and explain options for treating it.
6. Distinguish between the cancers that can occur in the male reproductive system.
7. Apply critical thinking skill Level 2, Comprehension.

PRIMARY AND SECONDARY SEXUAL CHARACTERISTICS

As was discussed in the previous chapter, primary sexual characteristics are directly involved in reproductive function. Even though the penis serves as the conduit for urination, it is seen as a primary sexual characteristic because it also serves the purpose of expelling semen (sperm and seminal fluid) into the vagina that may lead to procreation. Secondary sexual characteristics are physical aspects typically associated with one sex but not the other. Examples in men would be facial hair growth, deepening of the voice, increased body hair growth, and increased muscle development. All of these physical attributes occur during puberty by the production of testosterone, the hormone developed in abundance in the testes (Jones & Lopez, 2006).

SEXUAL/REPRODUCTIVE ANATOMY

Even though the female and male sexual/reproductive anatomies are perceived to be very different, these areas developed from the same embryonic tissue during pregnancy. Initial fetal genital formation occurs around eight to nine weeks after conception (Jones & Lopez, 2006). The process continues throughout the pregnancy until all internal and external structures are fully developed by thirty-eighth week of pregnancy (Heffner & Schust, 2006). Table 7.1 lists anatomically homologous structures shared between the two sexes.

TABLE 7.1: Homologous Anatomical Structures

MALE	FEMALE
Testes	Ovaries
Scrotum	Labia majora
Shaft of the penis	Labia minora
Glans of the penis	Glans of the clitoris
Foreskin	Clitoral hood
Cowper's gland	Bartholin's gland
Prostate gland	Skene's gland

EXTERNAL MALE GENITALIA

Unlike females in the United States who are more likely to have difficulty in recalling the clinical terms of their external genitalia, males find it easier remembering the clinical terms of their external male genitals than their internal reproductive anatomy. Even so, creative phrases abound to describe a male's external genitalia! For the majority of us, we call our hand, *hand*, our leg, *leg*, so why don't we all call the penis, *penis*?

THE PENIS

© 2011 by JM Travel Photography. Used under license of Shutterstock, Inc.

At birth, the penis consists of the shaft of the penis, the glans of the penis, the corona, the frenulum, and the foreskin. The penis is a rod-shaped male reproductive organ that passes semen and urine from the body (Jones & Lopez, 2006). It contains two types of spongy erectile tissue. The corpora cavernosa is two cylinders of erectile tissue that form most of the penis. The corpus spongiosum is a single column of erectile tissue that forms a small portion of the penis and surrounds the urethra (Ricci & Kyle, 2009). The erectile tissue is wrapped in connective tissue and covered with skin, but no pubic hair. The penis does not contain any bones or muscles. When a man is sexually aroused, nerve impulses from the autonomic nervous system dilate the arteries of the penis, allowing arterial blood to flow into the corpora cavernosa (Ricci & Kyle, 2009). The glans of the penis has thousands of nerve endings. At birth, the glans of the penis is covered with loose skin called the foreskin. The frenulum helps contract the foreskin over the glans. The corona is at the base of the glans of the penis, which forms a rounded projecting border. Over 60 percent of males in the United States (and around 30 percent globally) are circumcised, a procedure in which the foreskin and frenulum are removed, usually soon after birth. After a circumcision, the glans of the penis and corona remain permanently exposed.

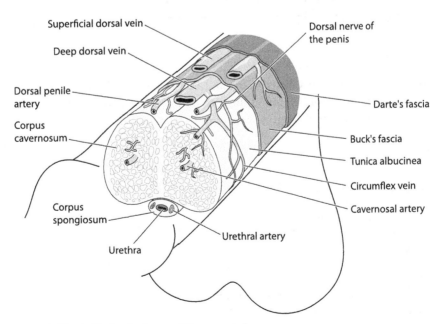

© 2011 by Blamb. Used under license of Shutterstock, Inc.

THE SCROTUM

Even though the scrotum is external, its purpose has to do with an internal reproductive organ. The scrotal sac regulates the temperature of and provides protection to the testicles (Ceo, 2006). Optimal temperature for sperm production is 94 degrees Fahrenheit. The scrotum does not hold the testes in place. The testes are suspended from the body wall by the spermatic cord (Jones & Lopez, 2006).

THE PERINEUM

The area of the perineum is located between the scrotum and the anus. It contains numerous nerve endings that indicate that it is sensitive to the touch (Ricci & Kyle, 2009). The perineum has nerves and blood vessels responsible for an erection. Prolonged pressure of this area from excessive amounts of time in the same position (such as on the saddle while cycling) can cause perineal numbness and damage to the blood vessels and nerves, which could lead to temporary erectile dysfunction (Dettori et al., 2004). The risk of erectile dysfunction can be reduced by adhering to these preventive strategies: (1) wearing padded bicycle shorts; (2) raising the handlebars to sit upright while riding a bicycle, which shifts the pressure from the perineum to the buttocks; (3) using a well-padded gel seat rather than a narrow one; and (4) positioning the seat so a man does not have to extend his legs fully at the bottom of his pedal stroke. Erectile dysfunction is discussed later in this chapter.

THE ANUS

The anus is the external opening of the rectum. As discussed in Chapter 6, there is no difference between a female and a male's anus. This area allows solid waste to be expelled from the body. The area has a relatively high concentration of nerve endings that suggest sensitivity to the touch. The anus does not contain glands to moisten the area so a water-based lubricant is required if penetration is expected.

INTERNAL MALE REPRODUCTIVE SYSTEM

THE TESTES

According to the American Congress of Obstetricians and Gynecologists, the testicles of a male fetus begin to descend from the abdomen into the scrotum around the fifth month of pregnancy (ACOG, 2010). This is the only organ located outside the body. Each testis begins sperm production and secretion of testosterone and estrogen at

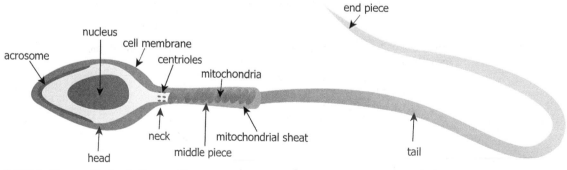

© 2011 by Zuzanae. Used under license of Shutterstock, Inc.

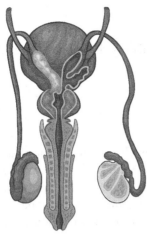

© 2011 by Qguz Aral. Used under license of Shutterstock, Inc.

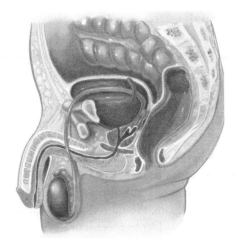

© 2011 by hkannn. Used under license of Shutterstock, Inc.

puberty. The production of testosterone and estrogen (which is mostly converted to testosterone) takes place in the tissue located between the seminiferous tubules (Krieger & Graney, 2008). Sperm is also produced in the seminiferous tubules within the testes (Krieger & Graney, 2008). On average, 1,000 sperm a second are produced from puberty until death. The entire process of sperm production takes 65 to 75 days (Jones & Lopez, 2006).

The average amount of sperm in an ejaculation is around 200 million, ranging from 40 million to 500 million. Only 1 percent of the seminal fluid ejaculated is sperm! The rest are substances (discussed below) needed for the maintenance, maturation, and transport of sperm (Jones & Lopez, 2006). If ejaculation occurs in a vagina, the sperm are viable for around five days in the female reproductive tract (Ricci & Kyle, 2009).

THE EPIDIDYMIS

The epididymis is located on the posterior side of the testes. Sperm are stored in the epididymis until ejaculation. Epididymal secretions help the sperm survive and mature as they undergo further stages of maturation. If this comma-shaped organ was stretched out, it would be almost 20 feet long (Ricci & Kyle, 2009). If ejaculation does not occur before more sperm are ready to enter the epididymis from the testes, they are reabsorbed into the body.

THE VAS DEFERENS

The vas deferens or vasa deferentia (plural) are coiled ducts (around 35 cm in length) that transport sperm from the epididymis to the seminal vesicles (Krieger & Graney, 2008). When a man wishes to be sterilized, each vas deferens is severed. This procedure is called a vasectomy (discussed in Chapter 8). There will not be any noticeable depletion in an ejaculation after a vasectomy because the seminal fluid in the semen is not affected. Seminal fluid is produced in the seminal vesicles, the prostate gland, and a small amount in the Cowper's gland (Ceo, 2006).

THE SEMINAL VESICLES

The seminal vesicles are glands (around 5 cm in length) that produce around 70 percent of the seminal fluid found in semen (Jones & Lopez, 2006). This substance contains water, is rich with sugar fructose and citric acid (both nutrients), and contains chemicals and enzymes that help neutralize the acidity in the male urethra and vagina, prolonging the lifespan of sperm.

THE EJACULATORY DUCT

The seminal fluid from the seminal vesicles is transported to the ejaculatory duct. These ducts (around 2 cm in length) deliver the seminal fluid to the prostate gland.

THE PROSTATE GLAND

The prostate gland (slightly larger than a chestnut) is in front of the rectum, located under the bladder. It completely encircles the urethra (Jones & Lopez, 2006). Around 30 percent of the seminal fluid is secreted by the prostate gland. Similar to the secretions from the seminal vesicles, this fluid helps neutralize the acidity of the urethra and the vagina. During an orgasm, the prostate gland contracts to propel the semen out of the penis and to close the part of the urethra by the bladder to prevent urine from being expelled during ejaculation (Krieger & Graney, 2008).

THE COWPER'S GLAND

The Cowper's gland is also called the bulbourethral gland. These pea-sized glands secrete a small amount of clear fluid when a male becomes sexually aroused (Krieger & Graney, 2008). Males may notice the fluid on the urethral opening at erection, right before ejaculation or not at all. This alkaline fluid is believed to coat the urethra before ejaculation to decrease the acidity of the urethra, which is mostly used for urination (and urine is acidic), and the vagina. This fluid can also carry live sperm to the urethral opening that were not expelled during a recent ejaculation (Jones & Lopez, 2006). Thus, caution should be taken if condoms are not used consistently or the withdrawal method is used for contraception.

ERECTILE DYSFUNCTION

Erectile dysfunction (also known as impotence) can be defined as the "inability to attain and/or maintain a penile erection sufficient for satisfactory sexual performance" (National Institute of Health Consensus Development Panel on Impotence, 1993). Failure to achieve an erection less than 20 percent of the time is not uncommon and treatment is rarely warranted. Experiencing erectile dysfunction (ED) more than 50 percent of the time, however, generally indicates there is a problem requiring medical attention. According to the National Institute of Health, around 5 percent of 40-year-old men and between 15 to 25 percent of 65-year-old men experience difficulty in achieving and/or maintaining an erection on a long-term basis.

Erective disorder can be classified into two types: acquired erectile disorder and lifelong erectile disorder. Acquired erectile disorder is applied to cases where the man has previously experienced erections, but for some reason is currently not able to maintain a functional erection. Men with lifelong erection disorder have never maintained a functional erection (Crooks & Baur, 2011).

There are various reasons why a man would experience erectile dysfunction: psychological distress, certain medications, cardiovascular disease, smoking, diabetes, and recovering from prostate cancer surgery are just a few. Moreover, erectile dysfunction has been found to be a symptom to a serious underlying medical condition, such as cardiovascular disease (Pohjantähti-Maaroos & Palomäki, 2011). Thus, screening for cardiovascular risk factors should be considered in men with ED, because symptoms of erectile dysfunction present on average three years earlier than symptoms of coronary artery disease (Heidelbaugh, 2010).

Any man, regardless of age, who is experiencing ED needs to be seen by a doctor to rule out or confirm any underlying medical problems. According to Heidelbaugh (2010), initial diagnostic workup should include a fasting serum glucose level and lipid panel, thyroid-stimulating hormone test, and morning total testosterone level. Lifestyle changes may also be necessary to regain the ability to attain and maintain erections. For example, obesity, sedentary lifestyle, and smoking greatly increase the risk of ED (Heidelbaugh, 2010). To prevent erectile dysfunction, men must make lifetime changes early enough to prevent irreversible changes in the arteries and nerves required for normal sexual functioning (Hales, 2011).

Three conditions must occur for an erection to be achieved and maintained. First, the nerves to the penis must be functioning properly. Second, the blood flowing into the penis must be adequate and remain within the penis when an erection is wanted. Third, the man must be sexually aroused—either through indirect stimulation or direct stimulation (Pohjantähti-Maaroos & Palomäki, 2011). With indirect stimulation, a man's genitals are not being touched. His brain is being stimulated by what a man identifies as sexually arousing to him either by sight, sound, or smell. With direct stimulation, a man's genitals are being touched and he finds this physical contact sexually arousing. If any of the three conditions is not met, though, then a man will have difficulty in attaining and/or maintaining an erection.

For the first condition, certain surgical procedures to remove the prostate gland have a high risk of damaging the nerves in the perineum that assist in erections. For men with prostate cancer (discussed later in this chapter), the "gold standard" in reducing the risk of the cancer from spreading to vital organs is to remove the prostate gland (which is known as radical prostatectomy). Unfortunately, erectile dysfunction remains the most commonly reported problem following such a procedure (Penson et al., 2005). For the second condition, certain diseases, such as diabetes and cardiovascular disease, prevent the smooth muscles in the penis from relaxing, thus allowing blood to leave the penis during an erection. This condition is known as a venous leak. For the third condition, if a man is not receiving adequate stimulation to sexually arouse him, then an erection will be difficult to attain and/or maintain.

There are currently five treatment options (not including sex therapy) available for erectile dysfunction (Albaugh, 2010). The first option includes medication taken in pill form (i.e., oral phosphodiesterase type 5 (PDE-5) inhibitors). These prescription-only drugs are more commonly known by their brand names: Viagra (sildenafil) by Pfizer, Levitra (vardenafil) by Bayer Pharmaceutical and Glaxo-Smith-Kline-Beecham/Schering Plough, and Cialis (tadalafil) by Lilly-ICOS. These drugs are taken when an erection is wanted, but the medication alone does not cause the erection. The drugs help the corpora cavernosa to engorge with blood when adequate sexual stimulation is provided (Heidelbaugh, 2010).

The second option is non-invasive and involves venous and vacuum constriction devices to retain blood in the penis during intercourse. An erection is produced through a suction chamber promoting penile blood engorgement and maintaining the erection with a constriction band at the base of the penis. This option includes the venous constriction loop and the vacuum constriction device (Heidelbaugh, 2010).

The third option is alprostadil, which is sold under the brand name Muse® (medicated urethral suppository for erection). With this prescription-only method, a man has to insert the medication (in suppository form) in the urethra at least ten minutes before an erection is needed. Alprostadil is a prostaglandin, a chemical produced naturally by the body to help regulate the contraction and relaxation of smooth muscle tissue (Althof et al., 2006). This chemical has been manufactured for erectile dysfunction to help relax the muscle tissue in the penis to allow blood to flow in to attain an erection. Adequate sexual stimulation will also help maintain an erection with this approach.

The fourth option to treat erectile dysfunction involves penile injections (Heidelbaugh, 2010). Men using this method need to integrate the injections into their sexual relationship. Erections after an injection can last about 30 to 60 minutes. The goal of penile injections is to produce an erection sufficient for penetration with the least amount of untoward side effects (Albaugh & Ferrans, 2010). Side effects include pain at the injection site and priapism (an erection lasting three hours or more).

The fifth and final option is a penile prosthesis device or penile implant (Heidelbaugh, 2010). Penile implants have been an option available to men with ED since 1973 (Quallich, Ohl, & Dunn, 2008). This is seen as the last option if all other available approaches were not successful in treating erectile dysfunction. A penile prosthesis consists of a pair of inflatable cylinders that are surgically implanted with the shaft of the penis. These cylinders are connected to a separate reservoir of fluid that has been surgically inserted under the groin muscles. A pump is also connected that allows the cylinders in the penis to fill with fluid to mimic an erection. This pump is placed in the scrotum. To obtain an erection, the man presses on the pump. The pump fills the cylinders with fluid from the reservoir causing an erection. To get rid of the erection, the man presses on a deflation valve located at the base of the pump. This will return the fluid to the reservoir and return the penis to a normal flaccid state. This treatment is associated with permanent damage to the normal erectile cylinders. Thus, spontaneous erections will no longer be possible (Heidelbaugh, 2010). Even though this method is the most invasive, it also has the highest satisfaction rates of all available treatments (Liechty & Quallich, 2008).

CANCER OF THE MALE REPRODUCTIVE SYSTEM

Along with prostate cancer, cancer of the penis and testicles are also possible. Only penile cancer is known to be primarily caused by HPV. Prostate and testicular cancers have other risk factors.

CANCER OF THE PROSTATE

When men think about cancer, many think of prostate cancer. There's no surprise there, because one in six men will be diagnosed with prostate cancer, but most of them will be over the age of 65. More than 2 million men in the United States who have been diagnosed with prostate cancer at some point are still alive today.

Prostate Symbol

Other than skin cancer, prostate cancer is the most common cancer in American men. The latest American Cancer Society (2010) estimates for cancer of the male reproductive organs in the United States are for 2010. For prostate cancer, about 217,730 were diagnosed and about 32,050 men died from it. Prostate cancer is the second leading cause of cancer death in American men, behind only lung cancer. The risk of prostate cancer is 1 in 6 and the risk of death due to metastasis is 1 in 30 (American Cancer Society, 2010).

According to Hales (2011), the risk of prostate cancer increases with age, family history, exposure to heavy metal cadmium, high number of sexual partners, and history of frequent sexually transmitted infections. The disease is more prevalent in African-American men than Caucasian men. Several theories abound. A diet high in saturated fats may be a risk factor, as well as an inherited predisposition, which may account for 5 to 10 percent of cases.

Prostate cancer can be detected by taking a simple annual screening test that measures levels of a protein called prostate-specific antigen (PSA) in the blood. African-American men with close relatives with prostate cancer are at high risk and therefore should be tested regularly after the age of 50.

Treatment may include hormone therapy, chemotherapy, a low fat diet, and radiation. Some treatments have proven effective in increasing the five-year survival rate from 67 to 99 percent over the past 26 years (Hales, 2011).

CANCER OF THE TESTICLES

About 8,480 new cases of testicular cancer were diagnosed and about 350 men died from it (American Cancer Society, 2010). The rate of testicular cancer has been increasing in many countries, including the United States. The increase is mostly in the cancer originating in the seminiferous tubules (called seminoma). Experts have not been able to find reasons for this increase, though.

Most cancers occur in individuals over the age of 55. Yet, testicular cancer is the most common form of cancer in men between the ages of 15 and 35 (American Cancer Society, 2010). The main risk factors for testicular cancer are family history and being born with undescended testes (the testicles remain in the abdomen at birth). There is a slow-growing form of testicular cancer (seminoma) usually found in men in their thirties and forties (American Cancer Society, 2010). Even so, testicular cancer is not common compared to other types of cancer. A man's lifetime chance of developing testicular cancer is about 1 in 300. In 2011, the U.S. Preventive Services Task Force (USPSTF) reaffirmed its 2004 recommendation against screening for testicular cancer in adolescent and adult males without any symptoms. Because treatment is so successful, the risk of dying from this cancer is very low—about 1 in 5,000. Radiation and chemotherapy have been very successful in keeping this cancer from spreading. If necessary, a testicle will be surgical removed, a procedure called an orchiectomy.

Symptoms include discomfort or pain in the testicle, or a feeling of heaviness in the scrotum, pain in the back or lower abdomen, enlargement of a testicle or a change in the way it feels, and lump or swelling in either testicle.

CANCER OF THE PENIS

About 1,250 new cases of penile cancer were diagnosed and an estimated 310 men died from it in 2010 (American Cancer Society, 2010). Penile cancer is very rare in North America and Europe. It accounts for less than 1 percent of cancers in men in the United States. This cancer occurs in about 1 man in 100,000 in the United States. However, penile cancer is much more common in some parts of Asia, Africa, and South America, where it accounts for up to 10 percent of cancers in men. Risk factors of penile cancer are HPV infection and not being circumcised.

CANCERS IN BOTH WOMEN AND MEN LINKED TO HPV

HPV oral infection is mainly sexually acquired and the recent increase in the incidence of oral cancers (or oropharyngeal carcinoma) has been considered the result of changing sexual behaviors (Chaturvedi et al., 2008). Not only are more couples in the United States participating in fellatio (mouth to penis) or cunniligus (mouth to vulva), but they are also not taking precautions to limit their exposure to the genital skin or vaginal/seminal secretions (Kreimer et al., 2005). Precautions need to be taken when participating in sexual activities that increase fluid transmission. A condom should be worn on a penis (there are condoms specifically made for oral sex) if fellatio is expected. A condom can also be cut in half lengthwise (cut off the tip first), opened up, and used on the vulva if cunnilingus will be performed.

For over a decade, the incidence of anal cancer has been increasing in women and men who participate in anal intercourse. There is a growing body of evidence to support the role of HPV in this disease (Balasubramanian, Palefsky & Koutsky, 2008). Receptive partners in anal sex are more at risk of acquiring HPV, but that does not mean insertive partners cannot be infected. Safer sex practices must be performed consistently in order to reduce the risk of HPV infection. Condoms worn for coitus can also be used for anal penetration. Moreover, the anus does not lubricate naturally, so a water-based lubricant is needed to prevent abrasions and tearing of the skin surrounding the anus, which could increase HPV infection.

REFLECTIONS

The purpose of this chapter was to familiarize students with the male sexual/reproductive anatomy. Many men are unacquainted with their internal reproductive structures. Why do you think there may be individuals in your class who do not know some of the terms for the internal male sexual/reproductive anatomy? When do you think this information should be taught, and by whom? Gaining knowledge and understanding of our bodies can be an important aspect of men's sexual well-being and sexual intelligence.

CRITICAL THINKING SKILL

Level 2, Comprehension. Demonstrate understanding of facts and ideas by organizing, comparing, translating, interpreting, giving descriptions, and stating main ideas.

Bloom's Taxonomy Key Words. Compare, extend, rephrase, contrast, associate, discuss, explain, rewrite, summarize, and provide examples.

CRITICAL THINKING QUESTIONS

1. How can men decrease their risk to cancer in their reproductive organs?
2. Around 60 percent of males in this country are circumcised at birth. European countries rarely modify the genitals of their babies. Why do you think we do?
3. The majority of women and men who participate in anal or oral sex do not protect their genitals to reduce the risk of HPV infection. Why do you think that is the case? How can society increase the use of condoms during these practices to reduce the exposure of HPV and other STIs?

WEBSITES

www.goofyfootpress.com

The Guide to Getting It On is a lighthearted approach to sexual topics.

www.womenshealth.gov/mens-health/sexual-health-for-men/

The Women's Health website has a section for men as well.

www.cdc.gov/cancer/

This site features current information on cancer of the breast, cervix, prostate, skin, and colon.

REFERENCES

Albaugh, J. (2010). Addressing and managing erectile dysfunction after prostatectomy for prostate cancer. *Urologic Nursing, 30*(3), 167–178.

Albaugh, J., & Ferrans, C. (2010). Impact of penile injections on men with erectile dysfunction after prostatectomy. *Urologic Nursing, 30*(1), 64–77.

Althof, S., O'Leary, M., Cappelleri, J., Crowley, A., Tseng, L., & Collins, S. (2006). Impact of erectile dysfunction on confidence, self-esteem and relationship satisfaction after 9 months of sildenafil citrate treatment. *Journal of Urology, 176*(5), 2132–2137.

American Cancer Society. (2010). *Cancer facts and figures, 2010.* Atlanta, GA: American Cancer Society.

American Congress of Obstetricians and Gynecologists (2010). *How your baby grows during pregnancy.* Danvers, MA: The American College of Obstetricians and Gynecologists.

Balasubramanian, A., Palefsky, J., & Koutsky, L. (2008). Cervical neoplasia and other STD-related genital tract neoplasias. In K. Holmes, P. Sparling, W. Stamm, P. Piot, J. Wasserheit, L. Corey, & M. Cohen (eds.), *Sexually Transmitted Diseases*, 4th ed., pp. 1051–1074. New York, NY: McGraw-Hill.

Ceo, P. (2006). Assessment of the male reproductive system. *Urologic Nursing, 26*(4), 290–296.

Chaturvedi, A., Engels, A., Anderson, F., & Gillison, M. (2008). Incidence trends for human papillomavirus-related and -unrelated oral squamous cell carcinomas in the United States. *Journal of Clinical Oncology, 26*, 612–619.

Crooks, R. & Baur, K. (2011). *Our sexuality*, 11th ed. Belmont, CA: Wadsworth/Cengage Learning.

Dettori, J., Koepsell, T., Cummings, P., & Corman, J. (2004). Erectile dysfunction after a long-distance cycling event: Associations with bicycle characteristics. *The Journal of Urology, 172*(2), 637–641.

Hales, D. (2011). *An invitation to health: Choosing a change*. Belmont, CA: Wadsworth/Cengage Learning.

Hatcher, R., Trussell, J., Stewart, F., Nelson, A., Cates, W., Guest, F., & Kowal, D. (2004). *Contraceptive Technology*, 18th ed. New York, NY: Ardent Media.

Heffner, L., & Schust, D. (2006). *Reproductive systems at a glance* (2nd ed.). Ames, IA: Blackwell Publishing Professional.

Heidelbaugh J. (2010). Management of erectile dysfunction. *American Family Physician, 81*(3), 305–312.

Jones, R., & Lopez, K. (2006). *Human reproductive biology*, 3rd ed. Burlington, MA: Elsevier.

Kreimer, A., CliVord, G., Boyle, P., & Franceschi, S. (2005). Human papillomavirus types in head and neck squamous cell carcinomas worldwide: A systematic review. *Cancer Epidemiology Biomarkers & Prevention, 14*, 467–475.

Krieger, J., & Graney, D. (2008). Clinical anatomy and physical examination of the male genital tract. In K. Holmes, P. Sparling, W. Stamm, P. Piot, J. Wasserheit, L. Corey, & M. Cohen (Eds.), *Sexually Transmitted Diseases*, 4th ed., 917–928. New York, NY: McGraw-Hill, Inc.

Liechty A., & Quallich, S. (2008). Teaching a patient to successfully operate a penile prosthesis. *Urologic Nursing, 28*(2), 106–108.

Penson, D., McLerran, D., Feng, Z., Li, L., Albertsen, P., Gilliland, F., & Stanford, J. (2005). 5-year urinary and sexual outcomes after radical prostatectomy: Results from the prostate cancer outcomes study. *The Journal of Urology, 173*(5), 1701–1705.

Pohjantähti-Maaroos, H., & Palomäki, A. (2011). Comparison of metabolic syndrome subjects with and without erectile dysfunction—Levels of circulating oxidised LDL and arterial elasticity. *International Journal of Clinical Practice, 65*(3), 274–280.

Ricci, S., & Kyle, T. (2009). *Maternity and pediatric nursing*. Philadelphia, PA: Lippincott Williams & Wilkins.

Quallich, S., Ohl, D., & Dunn, R. (2008). Evaluation of three penile prosthesis pump designs in a blinded survey of practitioners. *Urologic Nursing, 28*(2), 101–105.

CHAPTER

8

Contraception

CALCULATING YOUR REPRODUCTIVE YEARS

So . . . how many kids do you want to have? What age would you like to begin, and what age would you like to be done having kids? Many of us do not give it much thought, especially if we are young, haven't finished school, are barely starting out on our own, or are not in a committed relationship.

Let's just say that a woman wants to start having kids at the age of 25, which just happens to be the average age women in the United States start having kids (Martin et al. 2009). Let's also say that this woman started participating in coitus around the age of 17, which, in this country, is the average age for women (The Alan Guttmacher Institute, 2002). So, from 17 to 24 or 25, what contraceptive methods do you think she used *not* to get pregnant? Remember, "hope" is not a reliable contraception!

According to the Alan Guttmacher Institute (2000), on average, women in this country want to have only two children. Let's say a woman has had both her children by age 30 and does not want to have any more. Now what? She's "done"; does she still have to worry about getting pregnant again? Yes, she does, but for how long? As discussed in Chapter 5, most women won't go through menopause until around the age of 50. What will she do for the next *20 years* now that she is done having all the kids she wants to have? Sexual abstinence is an option, but not a very realistic one.

If you think that's crazy, let's figure out how many years men are fertile. Let's say a man was done having kids by the age of 35. Because the majority of men's testicles never stop producing sperm after puberty (Jones & Lopez, 2006), he is still fertile until he dies, which in this country is around the age of 75 for men (Xu et al., 2010). That means he still has *40 years* to *not* get a woman pregnant if he doesn't want to become a father again!

CONTRACEPTION

There are really only two reliable contraceptive methods available for men—condoms and male sterilization (these methods will be discussed at length later in this chapter). The contraceptive methods available for women, though, are abundant and vary considerably in time spent in using them and cost. Women can now choose from hormonal methods that come in the form of an injection, a patch, a vaginal ring, an implant, and an intra-uterine device (IUD), as well as non-hormonal methods. This chapter will discuss all of them.

TOP TWO CONTRACEPTIVE METHODS IN THE UNITED STATES

The top two contraceptive methods in the United States since 1982 have been oral contraceptives (known as "the pill") and female sterilization (The Alan Guttmacher Institute, 2010). The pill, a hormonal method that is reversible (i.e., a woman can stop taking it and get pregnant), is taken by almost 11 million women, and female sterilization, which is permanent (i.e., this method is meant to ensure a woman never gets pregnant again) has been used by over 10 million women (Mosher & Jones, 2010). Women who are childless are more likely to use the pill than sterilization as their form of contraception, whereas women who have three or more children are more likely to be sterilized than be on oral contraceptives (Mosher & Jones, 2010).

HOW HORMONAL METHODS PREVENT A PREGNANCY

As a hormonal method, the pill may contain estrogen and progestin (a synthesized version of progesterone) or only progestin. There is no pill (or any other contraceptive method) that just contains estrogen. The estrogen in the pill inhibits ovulation (Nelson, 2007). Ovulation does not occur because the low levels of estrogen in most hormonal contraceptive methods prevent the pituitary gland from releasing luteinizing hormone (LH). As was discussed in Chapter 6, LH is needed for ovulation to occur. The progestin in the pill thickens a woman's cervical mucus (which creates a barrier to sperm so the sperm can't enter the uterus) and suppresses endometrial growth (that's why women on a hormonal method usually have lighter menstrual bleeding). Unfortunately, there is NO contraceptive method that is 100 percent effective, completely safe, with no side effects, reversible, separate from sexual activity, inexpensive, easy to obtain, usable by either sex, and not dependent on the user's memory (Crooks & Baur, 2011). Keep in mind that just as no two people tolerate the same medication the same, no two women or two men will necessarily exhibit the same side effects (if any) when using a particular contraceptive method.

LONG-ACTING REVERSIBLE CONTRACEPTIVES (LARCS)

Long-acting reversible contraceptive (LARC) methods are hormonal and non-hormonal options that are highly effective and reversible (a pregnancy is possible when the method is no longer being used). A great advantage to these methods is that women (none exist for men) do not have to rely (or rely at a small degree only) on their compliance or correct use (Trussell, 2007b). Currently, the United States has four LARC methods available—three are hormonally-based and one is not.

The only non-hormonal long-acting reversible contraceptive method is ParaGard®. This contraceptive is an intrauterine device (IUD) that stays in place in the uterus for up to ten years. It is the longest continuous use LARC method in the market. One of the hormonal LARCs is also an intrauterine device, called Mirena®. This intrauterine system stays in place in the uterus for up to five years. Another hormonal LARC is Implanon®, a subdermal (under the skin of a woman's inner arm) implant that can remain in place for up to three years. The last hormonal LARC is an injection given every 12 weeks, called Depo-Provera®. If a pregnancy is planned sooner rather than later, then the first three methods can be removed prior to their expiration. A woman on Depo-Provera® can stop getting the injections to regain her fertility. Each of these methods is described in detail next.

HORMONAL CONTRACEPTIVE METHODS

Hormonal contraceptive methods are very effective. Effectiveness can be defined as calculating how many pregnancies will occur in 100 couples who use that particular method for one year (Trussell, 2007b). The most effective methods have 1 to 2 pregnancies per 100 couples that consistently use that particular method per year. The least effective methods have 30 pregnancies per 100 couples per year. Most (hormonal) methods have an effectiveness rate of 99.9 percent, but these rates vary when human error is taken into account. Most pregnancies among contraceptive users are caused by inconsistent or incorrect use, not by a failure of the method itself (Trussell, 2007a). The less a person has to think about using a method to prevent a pregnancy, the more effective that method will be. We'll begin this section discussing the least effective method in the most effective category and we will conclude this section discussing the most effective hormonal contraceptive method currently available to women, but NOT the most effective contraception on the market!

THE PILL

In the 1960s, most oral contraceptives contained anywhere from 2.5 to 10 milligrams (mgs) of estrogen or progestin (Nelson, 2007). This hormonal contraceptive method has come a long way in the last 50 years. Now, most pills contain less than 1mg of estrogen or progestin. If a woman is on the pill, she can look at the wrapper or box to identify the exact dosage of estrogen and/or progestin. The names of these hormones differ, though, so instead of reading *estrogen*, she might read *ethinyl estradiol*, and instead of reading *progestin*, she might read one of eight words: *desogestrel, drospirenone, ethynodiol diacetate, levonorestrel, norethindrone, norethindrone acetate, norgestimate,* or *norgestrel.*

Most oral contraceptives come in a pack of 28 pills. There are 28 pills because the pill was developed to mimic an average woman's menstrual cycle to make it easier for women to accept this form of contraception in the 1960s. Twenty-one pills have estrogen and progestin or progestin-only (known as "active" days) and the last seven pills are placebo. The placebo pills do not have any hormones in it, but some brands do have iron in their placebo pills. It is during the seven placebo pills that a woman menstruates even though she usually will not menstruate for all seven days. Remember that with any hormonal method, a woman bleeds not because an ovum wasn't fertilized (especially since ovulation should not have occurred) but because the placebo pills do not contain any hormones to stop a woman's endometrial lining from growing or shedding (Nelson, 2007).

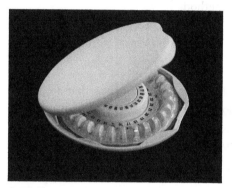

© 2011 by Jacob Kearns. Used under license of Shutterstock, Inc.

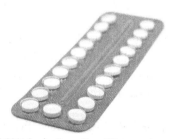

© 2011 by Anthony Shaw Photography. Used under license of Shutterstock, Inc.

© 2011 by Casablanka. Used under license of Shutterstock, Inc.

With oral contraceptives, women are supposed to take a pill every day, usually at the same time every day. For various reasons, women forget to take a pill (or two) during the 21-day "active" period. That is why this method is considered the least effective of the most effective. Many of us may not understand how difficult it is to take one small pill every day. Yet many women have complex lives with work, school, and family obligations competing for their time. Moreover, women may not appreciate the need for the constant hormonal balance that taking the pill every day at the same time provides. This indifference is more apparent if women never ingest the placebo pills.

A woman really doesn't have to take the placebo pills because they are mostly there to help a woman remember that she will be getting her period soon and when she needs to start a new pack. When some women decide not to take the placebo pills, they unfortunately may also forget to start a new pack. With seven placebo days and a few extra days with no intake of hormones from the pill, a woman's body starts resorting back to its old self and she may ovulate, even if she starts a new pack (Baerwald, Olatunbosun, & Pierson, 2006). This event is called *escape ovulation* (Willis et al., 2006). That's why you may have heard that some women have gotten pregnant even though they were on the pill.

Also, remember that if a woman is on the pill (and probably any hormonal method) and taking antibiotics, she needs to use a backup method for that month because this type of medication can interfere with a woman's body's ability in metabolizing the pill. Ovulation can occur and increase the risk of an ovum being fertilized by a sperm and implanting itself in the endometrial lining (Nelson, 2007). A woman should not stop taking the pill for that month, though. She may start bleeding when she was not supposed to and then find it a bit difficult to know when she needs to start a new pack. If her male partner isn't already doing so, he should wear a condom during that month to provide the protection needed to prevent an unintended pregnancy, as well as to reduce both their risk of any sexually transmitted infection (STI).

To decrease the incidence of escape ovulation, new oral contraceptives have been developed with more "active" pills and less placebo pills. Some pills (such as Loestrin 24Fe® and Yaz®) now have 24 instead of 21 pills with estrogen and progestin and 4 instead of 7 pills with placebo (Willis et al., 2006). This will hopefully reduce the amount of women who get pregnant while on the pill, but women still need to remember to take the pill every day around the same time! According to the FDA, unlike other oral contraceptives, Yasmin® and Yaz® contain the progestin drospirenone, which may increase potassium levels that could cause serious health complications. These oral contraceptives are not recommended for women who have ever had kidney, liver, or adrenal gland diseases.

There are oral contraceptives that are considered extended-cycle pills because a woman continues to take active pills past the usual 21 days of most oral contraceptives. For example, women on Seasonale® take a pill for 84 consecutive days with estrogen and progestin and 7 placebo pills (Anderson, Gibbons & Portman, 2006). Such a pill means that a woman will bleed once every three months (or once a season). Some women reported unscheduled withdrawal bleeding (i.e., spotting between periods) and thus, a similar pill was created to help eliminate such events (van Heusden & Fauser, 2002). This pill, called Seasonique®, has 84 "active" days and 7 low-dose estrogen pills. There are no placebo pills, but because the last 7 days do not contain progestin (which helps thin out the endometrial lining), a woman should experience bleeding only during that timeframe.

Another oral contraceptive relatively new to the market, called Lybrel®, has 28 pills with estrogen and progestin and no placebo pills. With no placebo pills, a woman does not bleed at all because this pill does not allow her endometrial lining to grow. If the endometrium doesn't grow, there's nothing to shed. Many women see menstrual bleeding as a sign that they are not pregnant. Even though using the pill (or any hormonal method) correctly should be enough to make women feel at ease, that is not the case for many women. Moreover, some women worry that not bleeding at all on a monthly basis is not healthy or natural. Research studies (Anderson, Gibbons & Portman, 2006) have reported that concern to be unfounded, but if a woman does not feel comfortable in not bleeding on a monthly basis, then Lybrel® is not the pill for her.

Women who cannot tolerate estrogen in oral contraceptives or are breastfeeding should not be on a hormonal contraceptive method with estrogen (Nelson, 2007). Breastfeeding mothers on a hormonal method with estrogen will have the hormone transferred to the breast milk and ingested by the infant. There is a pill that only has progestin in it, known as the mini-pill. The mini-pill is believed to be around 95 percent effective, though, so the utmost compliance in taking the mini-pill is needed (Raymond, 2007b).

Even though the majority of them are not serious, there are withdrawal symptoms a woman should be aware of when on a hormonal contraceptive method (Sulak et al., 2000). They include:

- Nausea
- Weight gain
- Sore or swollen breasts
- Unscheduled withdrawal bleeding
- Lighter menstrual periods
- Mood changes

There are over 100 oral contraceptives available, so a woman can ask her doctor to switch her to a different pill if the symptoms she is experiencing are disconcerting. Other side effects are rare but quite serious if they occur. Some of these symptoms may indicate a serious health complication like liver disease, stroke, blood clots, high blood pressure or heart disease (Nelson, 2007). Many of these conditions are not caused by being on a hormonal method, though. Even so, the following side effects can be remembered by the word "ACHES":

A – Abdominal (stomach) pain
C – Chest pain
H – Headaches (severe)
E – Eye problems (blurred vision)
S – Swelling and/or aching in the legs or thighs

If a woman is a smoker or over the age of 35, she needs to speak to her doctor about her contraceptive options because most women who fall in one of these two categories are not recommended to take a hormonal method containing estrogen. Hormonal contraceptives should not be considered as an option in women who have experienced blood clots in the arms, legs and lungs (and it should be discussed with her doctor if a first-degree relative did); serious heart and liver disease; or cancer of the breast or uterus. These women should also speak to their doctor about the possibility of carrying a pregnancy to term in the future because a pregnancy can make these conditions worse. The FDA encourages women who have experienced negative side effects of prescription drugs to visit www.fda.gov/medwatch or call 1-800-FDA-1088.

THE PATCH

The Ortho Evra Patch® is a hormonal contraceptive that is worn on a woman's skin. The only exception is the breasts because that part of the body usually has too much fatty tissue that doesn't allow the hormones to be adequately absorbed into the bloodstream. The hormones (both estrogen and progestin) are in the "sticky part" of the patch and a woman is given three patches in one packet and she changes the patch once a week for three weeks. On the fourth week she does not wear a patch and she will get her period. According to Mosher and Jones (2010), the percentage of women who had ever used the Ortho Evra Patch® rose from 1 percent in 2002 to 10 percent (5.3 million) in 2006–2008. Besides discussing this option with her doctor, a woman can always check the manufacturer's website at www.orthoevra.com for more information.

© 2011 by Tomasz Trojanowski. Used under license of Shutterstock, Inc.

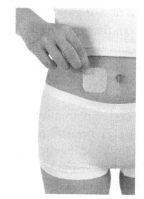

© 2011 by Tomasz Trojanowski. Used under license of Shutterstock, Inc.

© 2011 by Tomasz Trojanowski. Used under license of Shutterstock, Inc.

THE VAGINAL RING

The NuvaRing® is a hormonal contraceptive ring (about the size of a silver dollar) that a woman inserts into her vagina and places by her cervix. Before you think this is a daunting task, remember that a woman's vagina is not an endless tunnel—she will get to the end sooner than she thinks! She will leave the ring in place for three weeks. Even though for most women it will not fall out, if she feels it in her vagina then she hasn't put it in as far as it can go. On the fourth week she does not wear a vaginal ring and she will get her period. To help a woman remember how long she's had the vaginal ring inside her and when to put in a new one, her doctor will give her a digital hourglass that will help her keep track. Each NuvaRing® packet will come with stickers that she can place on her calendar to remember when she put the vaginal ring in and when she needs to take it out. Besides discussing this option with her doctor, a woman can always check the manufacturer's website at www.nuvaring.com for more information.

THE SHOT

Depo-Provera® is a hormonal contraceptive injection that a woman gets every 12 weeks. This contraception does not contain any estrogen; it is progestin only. Because of this, most women will cease menstruating completely after

6 to 12 months of being on this method (Goldberg & Grimes, 2007). Menstrual bleeding will return anywhere from three to six months after stopping this hormonal method. This method may also decrease the calcium in a woman's bones (Goldberg & Grimes, 2007). A woman on Depo-Provera® should take a calcium supplement and exercise to help defray calcium loss. These side effects are completely reversed when a woman stops using this method (Trussell, 2007b). Besides discussing this option with her doctor, a woman can always check the manufacturer's website at www.pfizer.com/products/rx/rx_product_depo_provera.jsp for more information.

IMPLANTS

Implanon® is a hormonal contraceptive that is a small rod (2 mm in diameter and 40 mm in length) implanted under the skin of a woman's inner arm by a doctor (Raymond, 2007a). The implant provides three years of contraceptive protection. Even though it lasts for three years, a woman can have the implant removed at any time before then if she decides to plan a pregnancy earlier than previously anticipated. This contraception does not contain any estrogen; it is progestin only. Because this method has to be implanted under the skin (a procedure that takes less than five minutes), the doctor needs to be trained. A woman can ask her doctor if she/he is trained and offers this method in the practice. She can always learn more about this contraception by visiting the manufacturer's website at www.implanon-usa.com for more information. The United Kingdom has recently taken Implanon® off the market because of a higher-than-expected incidence of pregnancies with this method.

Nexplanon® is similar to Implanon®, but not available in the United States. The difference between the two is that the Nexplanon applicator is designed for ease of insertion and the rod is radiopaque (does not let X-rays or other types of radiation penetrate) so it is easily identifiable. To learn more about this contraception, visit the manufacturer's website at www.nexplanontraining.co.uk/FAQ.aspx for more information.

Jadelle® is a hormonal contraceptive that is two small rods (approximately 2.5 mm in diameter and 43 mm in length) implanted under the skin of a woman's inner arm by a doctor. The implants provide five years of contraceptive protection (Raymond, 2007a). Unfortunately, this method is currently not available in the United States. To learn more about this contraception, visit the Population Council's website at www.popcouncil.org/what/jadelle.asp for more information.

INTRA-UTERINE SYSTEM (IUS)

Mirena® is a hormonal contraceptive this is inserted in a woman's uterus by a doctor. This is done by inserting the T-shaped device (around the size of a quarter) in the vagina, then the cervix to the uterus (Grimes, 2007). A woman is usually not given general anesthesia for this procedure. Local anesthesia is very possible, though. Most women are asked to take an over-the-counter pain reliever before the procedure. Insertion takes place when a woman is menstruating because the cervical os is slightly open to allow menstrual flow (Grimes, 2007). This contraception does not contain any estrogen; it is progestin only. The IUS can remain in the uterus for up to five years. To aid in detection and removal of the device, two white threads are tied through the tip. A doctor will cut the thread enough to have only a small amount protrude through the os. Similar to Implanon®, a woman can have the IUS removed before the five years if she decides to plan a pregnancy earlier than previously anticipated. The majority of gynecologists have been trained to insert Mirena®, so it should not be a problem finding a trained physician. Besides discussing this option with her doctor, a woman can always check the manufacturer's website at www.mirena-us.com for more information.

CHOOSING A HORMONAL METHOD

As you can see, women have a variety of hormonal methods to choose from. Men, though, currently do not have any hormonal contraceptive methods available for them. Why do you think that's the case? Given the choices available to women, and if a woman decides to use one of these options, she needs to ask herself which method seems right for her. Can she take a pill every day at the same time without forgetting? Would she prefer to get a shot every 12 weeks? Can she put her fingers in her vagina to insert the NuvaRing®? Does she mind having a patch on some part of her body and changing it once a week? Is she comfortable in having a device somewhere inside her body for years at a time? A woman needs to pick the method she can realistically and consistently use. If not, then it is not going to help prevent a pregnancy.

If a woman is a smoker, she should not be on any hormonal method with estrogen. Why? The pill adds a bit of stress to the blood vessels as it produces extra estrogen in the woman's body (Nelson, 2007). For a healthy woman, this should not be an issue of concern. For a woman who smokes, however, this increased stress is combined with what smoking does to the body. Nicotine causes high blood pressure and also increases the heart rate (Nelson, 2007). This puts stress on the blood vessels. Therefore, a woman who smokes while on a hormonal method with estrogen is overexerting her blood vessels in two ways. This combination can cause heart attacks, blood clots, and strokes. This becomes even more likely for women who are heavy smokers (smoking more than 15 cigarettes a day), as well as women over the age of 35.

Some women also change methods depending on their lifestyle. Maybe taking a pill every day is possible right now, but what if her work and home life become more demanding? Maybe she needs to switch to a method that she doesn't have to think about very often but is just as effective. Never forget that there is someone else that can help prevent a pregnancy, and that's the man she is sexually active with! Part of a healthy (heterosexual) sexual relationship is communicating about how to prevent unintended pregnancies together. Given the few contraceptive options available to men who are in sexual relationships with women, they need to realize that they are or will be surrendering their reproductive health to their female sexual partner. If men want to decide when they want to become fathers or not, they have to take a more active role in preventing unintended pregnancies by using condoms consistently or getting sterilized (the latter is usually not available to men younger than 25 and childless).

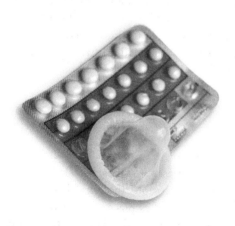

© 2011 by mick20. Used under license of Shutterstock, Inc.

There is no hormonal contraceptive method that reduces a person's risk of being infected by an STI (Marrazzo, Guest, & Cates, 2007). Besides trying to keep yourself from getting pregnant (or getting someone pregnant), you also need to reduce your risk of exposing yourself to an STI (discussed in Chapter 10). Along with being in a monogamous relationship with an uninfected partner, only barriers like the female and male condom can help reduce your risk. Using a hormonal and barrier method can improve the chances of preventing an unintended pregnancy and reducing one's risk to an STI. Keep in mind that some STIs can be passed on by skin-to-skin contact (meaning no seminal and/or vaginal fluid transmission is needed to become infected), like genital herpes and HPV (Marrazzo, Guest, & Cates, 2007). Women also need to remember that being on any hormonal method is considered taking some form of medication. So when a doctor asks her if she is on any medication, the hormonal contraceptive she is on counts!

NON-HORMONAL CONTRACEPTIVE METHODS

Non-hormonal contraceptive agents or devices work by preventing sperm from joining an ovum. Even though the majority of these methods are not as effective as hormonal options to prevent a pregnancy, the most effective method falls in this category, as do the permanent, non-reversible contraceptive choices currently available (Pollack, Thomas, & Barone, 2007). This section begins with the least effective method to prevent an unintended pregnancy and concludes with the most effective contraceptive in the market.

FERTILITY AWARENESS METHODS

Fertility awareness methods are considered the least effective in preventing unintended pregnancies because daily adherence is needed for continued protection. Some days out of the month are considered "non-coital" days; thus, spontaneous sexual activity is not always realistic and a woman's menstrual cycle can deviate from its normal schedule due to illness, medication, and stress (Jennings & Arevalo, 2007). Using more than one fertility awareness method concurrently can improve the chances of preventing an unintended pregnancy.

© 2011 by Anton Novik. Used under license of Shutterstock, Inc.

In using the Standard Days Method®, women follow their "safe" and "unsafe" days to participate in coitus by using CycleBeads®. CycleBeads® is a color-coded string of beads that represents the days of a woman's cycle. A woman moves a ring over the beads to track each day of her cycle. The color of the beads indicates whether a particular day may result in a pregnancy if coitus is initiated.

In using the cervical mucus ovulation detection, women check the quantity and quality of cervical mucus expelled from the vaginal opening with their fingers or tissue paper *every morning*. Cervical mucus changes in color and consistency throughout the menstrual cycle. Before ovulation, the mucus will be cloudy, white, or yellow and sticky. During ovulation, the mucus will be clear, wet, stretchy, sticky, and slippery (Jennings & Arevalo, 2007).

In using the basal body temperature method, women check their temperature *every day* before they get out of bed. A woman's body temperature rises as she nears ovulation. With this method, a woman is expected to refrain from coitus starting on the first day of her menstrual bleeding until she has documented three consecutive days of sustained body temperature (Jennings & Arevalo, 2007).

SPERMICIDES

Spermicide contains a chemical that kills sperm. This substance may be purchased in the form of foam, jelly, cream, suppository, or film that is placed inside the vagina before coitus. Some types must be put in place 30 minutes ahead of time (read the package for instructions). Spermicides have a higher unintended pregnancy rate than other barrier methods. Spermicides should always be used with another form of contraception, such as a condom, to increase protection. Keep in mind that frequent use may cause tissue (vaginal, cervical, or penile) irritation, which can increase the risk of vaginal infections and the transmission of sexually transmitted infections (STIs).

BARRIER METHODS

Barriers have been developed to prevent sperm from fertilizing an egg by either blocking the entrance to the cervix through a removable device surrounding the cervix or a sheath that covers the penis or vagina. Cervical devices currently available in the United States are the diaphragm, the cervical cap, Lea's shield, FemCap, and the contraceptive sponge. These cervical barriers allow seminal fluid to enter the vagina but the device covering the cervix does not allow the sperm to enter the upper reproductive tract.

CERVICAL BARRIERS

Diaphragms, Lea's shield, FemCap, and cervical caps must be fitted by an experienced health care provider and left in place by the cervix for six to eight hours after coitus. Some of these cervical barriers have to be inserted hours before coitus is anticipated. Thus, spontaneous sexual activity may be difficult with some of these methods. Condoms and the contraceptive sponge do not require a prescription. Barrier methods do not have many side effects, unless you or your sexual partner is allergic to the material (latex) some of these methods are made from.

FEMALE AND MALE CONDOMS

During coitus, physical barrier contraceptives such as the female and male condom prevent sperm from fertilizing an egg by blocking the presence of semen in the female lower reproductive tract (Warner & Steiner, 2007). After ejaculation, the semen remains within the sheath of either of these two methods.

Unlike all hormonal methods, condoms do not require a prescription and side effects are minimal. It is possible, though, for either sexual partner to have an allergic reaction to latex, the material that the majority of male condoms are made from. Female and some male condoms are made of polyurethane.

A new female condom has been developed from synthetic nitrile. A female condom is worn internally by the receptive partner to physically block semen from entering that person's body and can be worn up to eight hours before coitus. A male condom is worn on an erect penis to physically block his semen from entering another person's body during coitus, fellatio, or anal sex (Warner & Steiner, 2007).

© 2011 by nito. Used under license of Shutterstock, Inc.

© 2011 by Dino O. Used under license of Shutterstock, Inc.

If a condom is the method of contraceptive choice for a couple, a penis should never be near nor enter the vaginal opening unless a condom is worn by either partner. It is not recommended for both partners to have a condom on at the same time—the thrusting is believed to weaken the integrity of the condoms, thus increasing the risk of breakage.

COITUS INTERRUPTUS (WITHDRAWAL METHOD)

With the withdrawal method, the man does not ejaculate inside a woman's vagina during coitus. Recent research suggests that more couples use this method than previously documented (Jones et al., 2009). Even so, this method is not for the faint of heart, given a typical use failure rate of 18 percent, but ranging from 14 to 24 percent (Kost et al., 2008). Many couples report "pulling out" along with using another contraceptive method, like the pill or the condom (Jones et al., 2009).

INTRA-UTERINE DEVICE (IUD)

ParaGard® is an IUD that can be inserted into the uterus by a doctor. Unlike Mirena®, this method does not contain any hormones in it and can stay in place for up to ten years. ParaGard® has copper throughout and works by creating a hostile uterine environment to sperm. Besides discussing this option with her doctor, a woman can always check the manufacturer's website at www.paragard.com for more information.

GyneFix® is another IUD that can be inserted into the uterus by a doctor. It differs in shape and size when compared to ParaGard® or Mirena®. It does not have any "arms" (which give ParaGard® and Mirena® the "T" shape) and it is smaller in size. It does not contain any hormones and it can stay in place for up to five years. It is currently not available in the United States.

STERILIZATION

If a person has decided that he or she does not want to be fertile any longer, sterilization is an effective solution.

FEMALE STERILIZATION

Since 1982, female sterilization has been in the top two spots of one of the most widely used contraceptive methods in the United States. The percentage of women who rely on female sterilization as their form of contraception increases as a woman gets older (Mosher & Jones, 2010). There are two procedures to permanently cease a woman's ability to become pregnant: tubal ligation and hysteroscopic tubal sterilization, known as Essure® (Jones & Lopez, 2006).

With tubal ligation, the fallopian tubes are cut, burned, or blocked with rings, bands or clips. Carbon dioxide is pumped into the abdominal cavity to render the fallopian tubes more visible to the doctor performing the surgery (Jones & Lopez, 2006). A woman is usually given general anesthesia, but local anesthesia is on the rise, with many of these procedures taking place in an outpatient setting. A woman will experience pain, tenderness, and bloating for about a week after the surgery. The surgery is effective immediately.

For Essure®, a doctor inserts a coil through the vagina, cervix, and uterus and into the fallopian tubes. A camera is also inserted to help the doctor navigate through the vagina, cervix, and uterus into the fallopian tubes, as well as to provide immediate visual confirmation of placement. A woman is not given general anesthesia, but she does receive local anesthesia in the cervix. Most women will be asked to take an over-the-counter pain reliever before the procedure. She will probably feel cramping throughout the procedure and for a few hours afterward. During the three months following the procedure, the fallopian tubes form scar tissue around the inserted coil that prevents sperm from reaching the ovum. During this time, a woman must continue using another method of contraception to prevent a pregnancy. After three months, a woman gets an Essure Confirmation Test. This test is usually done in a hospital because it uses a dye and a special type of X-ray to ensure that the coils are in

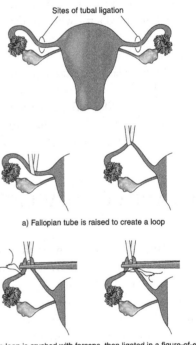

Sites of tubal ligation

a) Fallopian tube is raised to create a loop

b) The loop is crushed with forceps, then ligated in a figure-of-eight

c) The loop is excised at the crushed zone

© 2011 by Blamb. Used under license of Shutterstock, Inc.

place and that the fallopian tubes are completely blocked (Jones & Lopez, 2006). Besides discussing this option with her doctor, a woman can always check the manufacturer's website at www.essure.com for more information.

MALE STERILIZATION

A vasectomy is considered the most effective contraception available. It is the fourth most popular contraception in the United States (The Alan Guttmacher Institute, 2010). A vasectomy is a permanent form of contraception that prevents the release of sperm when a man ejaculates. During a vasectomy, the scrotal skin is cut, and the vas deferens located in each testicle is severed. The two ends of the vas deferens are tied, stitched, or sealed. Electrocautery (cutting with heat) may be used to seal the ends. Scar tissue from the surgery may also help block the tubes.

During this procedure, a man is given local anesthesia in each testicle. He is rarely, if ever, given general anesthesia. The procedure takes around 20 to 30 minutes. The man is asked to relax at home for the next two to three days and refrain from lifting anything heavy for one week. His testicles will ache and be tender, and he might experience scrotal swelling.

After a vasectomy, it usually takes around 15 to 20 ejaculations to completely clear sperm from the semen (Jones & Lopez, 2006). Thus, a man will have to use another form of reliable contraception for the first three months after the procedure. After three months (or 20 ejaculations, whichever come first), the man will be asked to go back to the doctor who performed the vasectomy to confirm that the reproductive tract has been cleared of sperm (Pollack, Thomas, & Barone, 2007). This is done by having the man ejaculate in a cup, and the seminal fluid is analyzed for the existence of sperm.

The testicles continue to produce sperm after a vasectomy, but the sperm are reabsorbed by the body. Sperm is also reabsorbed if ejaculation does not occur after a while, regardless of whether a male has had a vasectomy (Jones & Lopez, 2006). Because only 1 percent of ejaculation is sperm and the tubes are blocked before the seminal vesicles and prostate gland (where the majority of seminal fluid is produced), a man will still ejaculate about the same amount of fluid (Pollack, Thomas, & Barone, 2007).

MEN AND CONTRACEPTION

Because there are so many more contraceptive options for women and because society assumes women should take primary responsibility in preventing unintended pregnancies, many men may be ambivalent about their role in their own reproductive health. There are only three contraceptive options (and one of them is not considered as reliable) for men, and all are non-hormonal methods. Why do you think we have not developed reliable hormonal contraceptives for men?

Men will have to ask themselves which method seems right for them given their current circumstances. Are they currently in a casual relationship that deems condom use necessary? Is it possible to seriously consider condom use as the main form

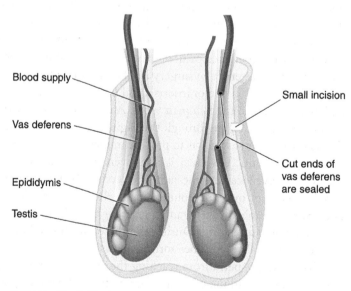

© 2011 by Blamb. Used under license of Shutterstock, Inc.

of contraception if the relationship is considered monogamous and long-term? Why or why not? What if a female sexual partner admits to be using a reliable form of contraception, like the pill: Will the man now surrender full responsibility of preventing an unintended pregnancy to her? What if he's 30 years old and has had all the children he wants to have: Would he seriously consider having a vasectomy?

EMERGENCY CONTRACEPTION

Emergency contraception works after coitus has occurred to help avoid an unintended pregnancy. This is an option if no contraceptive method was used or if a woman suspects her usual method failed. Plan B, Plan B One-Step, and a generic version of Plan B called Next Choice all contain a high dose of a progestin. Emergency contraception inhibits ovulation, thus decreasing the chance of fertilization from a specific coital act. Emergency contraception is *not* a form of abortion. On the contrary, it helps prevent abortion by preventing unintended pregnancies (Stewart, Trussell, & Van Look, 2007).

No prescription is needed for women aged 17 and older. Emergency contraception must be used within 120 hours of coitus. According to Mosher and Jones (2010), between 2002 and 2006–2008, the percentage of women who had ever used emergency contraception rose from 4 to 10 percent (5.2 million).

REFLECTIONS

The purpose of this chapter is to provide information about the variety of options available for preventing an unintended pregnancy. With an unplanned pregnancy rate of almost 50 percent in the United States (Ventura et al., 2009), a number of issues need to be addressed in order to increase the percentage of planned pregnancies while decreasing the incidence of unintended pregnancies. Obtaining reliable, medically accurate information on the contraceptive methods available in the United States is a good start to helping prevent unintended pregnancies and plan future pregnancies. Access to affordable and reliable contraceptive options to all women and men also needs to become a reality.

CRITICAL THINKING SKILL

Level 3, Application. Solve problems to new situations by applying acquired knowledge, facts, techniques and rules in a different way.

Bloom's Taxonomy Key Words. Prepare, demonstrate, examine, apply, interpret, modify, graph, and translate.

CRITICAL THINKING QUESTIONS

1. Other countries, such as Sweden, Denmark, the Netherlands, England, and France, have lower rates of unintended pregnancies than the United States. Why do you think that is?
2. How do you think access to reliable methods and comprehensive sexuality education, along with an awareness of adolescent sexuality, helps in preventing unintended pregnancies?
3. What role, if any, do you think religion played in your parents' contraceptive use? How about your own?
4. If there was a hormonal method, like the pill, for men, do you think they would take it? Why or why not? If such an option was available, do you think women would surrender control of their reproductive health to men? Why or why not?

WEBSITES

www.acha.org
American College Health Association

www.acog.org
American College of Obstetrics and Gynecology

www.asrm.org
American Society for Reproductive Medicine

www.cdc.gov
Centers for Disease Control and Prevention

www.cdc.gov/nchs
National Center for Health Statistics

www.nfprha.org/facts/contraception
National Family Planning and Reproductive Health Association

www.ppfa.org
Planned Parenthood Federation of America

www.siecus.org
Sexuality Information and Education Council of the United States (SICEUS)

REFERENCES

The Alan Guttmacher Institute (2010). *Facts on contraceptive use in the United States.* New York, NY: The Alan Guttmacher Institute.

The Alan Guttmacher Institute (2002). *In their own right: Addressing the sexual and reproductive health needs of American men.* New York, NY: The Alan Guttmacher Institute.

The Alan Guttmacher Institute (2000). *Fulfilling the promise: Public policy and U.S. family planning clinics.* New York, NY: The Alan Guttmacher Institute.

Anderson, F., Gibbons, W., & Portman, D. (2006). Safety and efficacy of an extended-regimen oral contraceptive utilizing continuous low-dose ethinyl estradiol. *Contraception, 73,* 229–234.

Baerwald, A., Olatunbosun, O., & Pierson, R. (2006). Effects of oral contraceptives administered at defined stages of ovarian follicular development. *Fertility & Sterility, 86,* 27–35.

Cates, W., & Raymond, E. (2007). Vaginal barriers and spermicides. In R. Hatcher, J. Trussell, A. Nelson, W. Cates, F. Stewart, & D. Kowal (eds.), *Contraceptive Technology,* 19th ed., pp. 317–336. New York, NY: Ardent Media.

Crooks, R., & Baur, K. (2011). *Our sexuality,* 11th ed. Belmont, Calif.: Wadsworth/Cengage Learning.

Goldberg, A., & Grimes, D. (2007). Injectable contraceptives. In R. Hatcher, J. Trussell, A. Nelson, W. Cates, F. Stewart, & D. Kowal (eds.), *Contraceptive Technology,* 19th ed., pp. 157–170. New York, NY: Ardent Media.

Grimes, D. (2007). Intrauterine devices (IUDs). In R. Hatcher, J. Trussell, A. Nelson, W. Cates, F. Stewart, & D. Kowal (Eds.), *Contraceptive Technology,* 19th ed., pp. 117-139. New York, NY: Ardent Media.

Hatcher R., & Brawner Namnoum, A. (2007). In R. Hatcher, J. Trussell, A. Nelson, W. Cates, F. Stewart, & D. Kowal (eds.), *Contraceptive Technology,* 19th ed., pp. 7–18. New York, NY: Ardent Media.

Jennings, V., & Arevalo, M. (2007). Family awareness-based methods. In R. Hatcher, J. Trussell, A. Nelson, W. Cates, F. Stewart, & D. Kowal (eds.), *Contraceptive Technology,* 19th ed., pp. 343–360. New York, NY: Ardent Media.

Jones, R., Fennell, J., Higgins, J., & Blanchard, K. (2009). Better than nothing or savvy risk-reduction practice? The importance of withdrawal. *Contraception, 79*, 407–410.

Jones, R., & Lopez, K. (2006). *Human Reproductive Biology*, 3rd ed. Burlington, MA: Elsevier.

Kowal, D. (2007). Coitus interruptus (withdrawal). In R. Hatcher, J. Trussell, A. Nelson, W. Cates, F. Stewart, & D. Kowal (Eds.), *Contraceptive Technology*, 19th ed., pp. 337–342. New York, NY: Ardent Media.

Marrazzo, J., Guest, F., & Cates, W. (2007). Reproductive tract infections, including HIV and other sexually transmitted infections. In R. Hatcher, J. Trussell, A. Nelson, W. Cates, F. Stewart, & D. Kowal (eds.), *Contraceptive Technology*, 19th ed., pp. 499–558. New York, NY: Ardent Media.

Martin, J., Hamilton, B., Sutton, P., Ventura, S., Menacker, F., Kirmeyer, S., & Mathews, T. (2009). Births: Final data for 2006. *National Vital Statistics Reports, 57*(7). Hyattsville, MD: National Center for Health Statistics.

Mosher, W., & Jones, J. (2010). Use of contraception in the United States: 1982–2008. *Vital Health Statistics, 23*(29). Hyattsville, MD: National Center for Health Statistics.

Nanda, K. (2007). Contraceptive patch and vaginal contraceptive ring. In R. Hatcher, J. Trussell, A. Nelson, W. Cates, F. Stewart, & D. Kowal (eds.), *Contraceptive Technology*, 19th ed., pp. 271–296. New York, NY: Ardent Media.

Nelson, A. (2007). Combined oral contraceptives. In R. Hatcher, J. Trussell, A. Nelson, W. Cates, F. Stewart, & D. Kowal (eds.), *Contraceptive Technology*, 19th ed., pp. 193–270. New York, NY: Ardent Media.

Pollack, A., Thomas, L., & Barone, M. (2007). Female and male sterilization. In R. Hatcher, J. Trussell, A. Nelson, W. Cates, F. Stewart, & D. Kowal (eds.), *Contraceptive Technology*, 19th ed., pp. 361–402. New York, NY: Ardent Media.

Raymond, E. (2007a). Contraceptive implants. In R. Hatcher, J. Trussell, A. Nelson, W. Cates, F. Stewart, & D. Kowal (eds.), *Contraceptive Technology*, 19th ed., pp. 145–156. New York, NY: Ardent Media.

Raymond, E. (2007b). Progestin-only pills. In R. Hatcher, J. Trussell, A. Nelson, W. Cates, F. Stewart, & D. Kowal (eds.), *Contraceptive Technology*, 19th ed., pp. 181–192. New York, NY: Ardent Media.

Stewart, F., Trussell, J., & Van Look, P. (2007). Emergency contraception. In R. Hatcher, J. Trussell, A. Nelson, W. Cates, F. Stewart, & D. Kowal (eds.), *Contraceptive Technology*, 19th ed., pp. 87–116. New York, NY: Ardent Media.

Sulak, P., Scow, R., Preece, C., Riggs, M., & Kuehl, T. (2000). Hormone withdrawal symptoms in oral contraceptive users. *Obstetrics & Gynecology, 95*, 261–266.

Trussell, J. (2007a). Choosing a contraceptive: Efficacy, safety and personal considerations. In R. Hatcher, J. Trussell, A. Nelson, W. Cates, F. Stewart, & D. Kowal (eds.), *Contraceptive Technology*, 19th ed., pp. 19–48. New York, NY: Ardent Media.

Trussell, J. (2007b). Contraceptive efficacy. In R. Hatcher, J. Trussell, A. Nelson, W. Cates, F. Stewart, & D. Kowal (eds.), *Contraceptive Technology*, 19th ed., pp. 747–756. New York, NY: Ardent Media.

van Heusden, A., & Fauser, B. (2002). Residual ovarian activity during oral steroid contraception. *Human Reproduction Update, 8*, 345–358.

Ventura, S., Abma, J., Mosher, W., & Henshaw, S. (2009). Estimated pregnancy rates for the United States, 1990–2005: An update. *National Vital Statistics Reports, 58*(4). Hyattsville, MD: National Center for Health Statistics.

Warner, L., & Steiner, M. (2007). Male condoms. In R. Hatcher, J. Trussell, A. Nelson, W. Cates, F. Stewart, & D. Kowal (eds.), *Contraceptive Technology*, 19th ed., pp. 297–316. New York, NY: Ardent Media.

Willis, S., Kuehl, T., Spiekerman, A., & Sulak, P. (2006). Greater inhibition of the pituitary-ovarian axis in oral contraceptive regimens with a shortened hormone-free interval. *Contraception, 74*, 100–103.

Xu, J., Kochanek, K., Murphy, S., Tejada-Vera, B. (2010). Deaths: Final data for 2007. *National Vital Statistics Reports, 58*(19). Hyattsville, MD: National Center for Health Statistics.

CHAPTER

9

Pregnancy

OBJECTIVES: STUDENTS WILL BE ABLE TO

1. Identify the possible outcomes of a pregnancy.
2. Recognize the hormones necessary to sustain a pregnancy.
3. Describe the three trimesters of pregnancy.
4. Detail the causes of maternal and infant deaths.
5. Apply critical thinking skill Level 4, Analysis.

PREGNANCY OUTCOMES

In the United States, an estimated 6 million women become pregnant annually (Martin et al., 2009). In any given year, around 10 percent of reproductive age women experience a pregnancy (Mosher & Jones, 2010). According to Ventura and her colleagues (2009), of the 6.4 million pregnancies in the United States in 2006, 4 million resulted in births, 1.3 million in abortions, and 1.1 million in miscarriages and stillbirths. The proportions of pregnancies that were intended (51 percent) and unintended (49 percent) were almost identical.

© 2011 by wavebreakmedia ltd. Used under license of Shutterstock, Inc.

© 2011 by Monkey Business Images. Used under license of Shutterstock, Inc.

PREGNANCY OUTCOME—BIRTH

Of the 3.3 million intended pregnancies in the United States in 2006, 80 percent resulted in births. Of the 3.1 million unintended pregnancies, 44 percent resulted in births (Ventura et al., 2009). A baby can be born through the vagina or through the abdomen via a cesarean section. Cesarean delivery involves major abdominal surgery and is associated with higher rates of surgical complications. In 2007, nearly one-third (32 percent) of all births were cesarean deliveries—the highest rate ever reported in the United States (Menacker & Hamilton, 2010). New Jersey had the highest rate at 38 percent, whereas Utah had the lowest rate at 22 percent. Even though women can request a c-section even if it's not medically necessary, most women have this procedure because they had a prior c-section (especially if it occurred less than five years ago), the fetus is not in a head-down position in the uterus during labor, the woman is experiencing a medical emergency, and/or the baby is under fetal distress. Moreover, pregnant women between 40 and 54 years old are more likely to have a c-section than any other age group (Menacker & Hamilton, 2010).

AGE AT FIRST BIRTH

The average age women are giving birth in this country is 25 years old. In 1970, the average age was 21 years old. In 2006, Asian/Pacific Islander women had the oldest average age at first birth (28.5 years) and American Indian/Alaska Native women had the youngest (21.9 years). Women postpone parenthood for various reasons, and more and more women are choosing to give birth for the first time later in life. With the advancements of assisted reproductive technology, many couples are able to begin a family in their thirties, forties, and even fifties! Keep in mind, though, that any pregnant woman 35 years or older is considered carrying a "high risk" pregnancy due to her age and the increased risk of pregnancy complications and negative outcomes (Brown, 2007).

PREGNANCY OUTCOME—ABORTION

Women do terminate a planned pregnancy, but the number is low and cannot be represented in percentage terms. Of the 3.1 million unintended pregnancies in the United States in 2006, though, 42 percent resulted in abortions (Ventura et al., 2009). The national average rate of abortion is 19.6 per 1,000 women. In 2008, Delaware had the highest rate of abortion (40 women per 1,000 women) and Wyoming had the lowest abortion rate, less than 1 per 1,000 women (Jones & Kooistra, 2011).

Eighty-eight percent of abortions occur in the first 12 weeks of pregnancy (Jones & Kooistra, 2011). The remaining 12 percent break down as follows: 6.6 percent of abortions occur during 13 to 15 weeks of pregnancy, 3.8 percent during weeks 16 to 20, and 1.5 percent occur at 21 weeks or more (The Guttmacher Institute, 2011). In 2000, the FDA approved mifepristone (also known by the trade name Mifeprex or its original French name, RU-486) for use along with a prostaglandin (a hormone that causes uterine contractions and softens the cervix) for terminating pregnancies up to 49 days from the onset of a woman's last menstrual period (Jones & Kenshaw, 2002). These early medication (nonsurgical) abortions accounted for 11 percent of all abortions in 2006 (Pazol et al., 2009). Around 88 percent of abortions were surgically performed by curettage (i.e., dilating the cervix and scraping the endometrial lining), along with vacuum or suction aspiration (i.e., removing uterine contents during the first trimester), or dilation and evacuation procedures (i.e., removing uterine contents during the second trimester).

The United States has one of the highest rates of abortions when compared to other developed countries (The Guttacher Institute, 2011). If reducing the amount of abortions in this country is a goal, then society needs to concentrate on reducing the number of unintended pregnancies experienced every year. Reducing access to and increasing barriers to abortion services and providers does not prevent the termination of pregnancies, but helping couples get pregnant only when they want to get pregnant will (Cohen, 2006).

PREGNANCY OUTCOME—FETAL LOSS

According to Ventura and her colleagues (2009), of the 3.3 million intended pregnancies in the United States in 2006, 20 percent resulted in fetal losses (miscarriage or stillbirth). Of the 3.1 million unintended pregnancies, 14 percent ended in fetal losses.

A miscarriage is defined as a spontaneous abortion that occurs before the twentieth week of pregnancy. Approximately one in four clinically recognized pregnancies end in miscarriage. It is considered the most common disorder of pregnancy. If miscarriages include a loss that occurs before a positive pregnancy test, then some estimate that 40 percent of all conceptions end in a miscarriage. The risk of miscarriage increases with a woman's age. For example, 30 to 50 percent of women over the age of 40 will miscarry, whereas 7 to 15 percent of women under the age of 30 will experience such a loss.

Even though there are a variety of reasons (biological and environmental) why a miscarriage occurs, more than one half of all miscarriages that happen during the first trimester are a result of chromosomal abnormalities affecting the fetus (Jones & Lopez, 2006). Miscarriages that transpire during the second trimester result from an incompetent (i.e., weak) cervix that cannot hold the weight of the pregnancy. To decrease the chance of a miscarriage due to an incompetent cervix, the American Pregnancy Association recommends women to consider having their cervix sewn during the pregnancy. This is called a cervical cerclage. A doctor will stitch a band of strong thread around the cervix, and the thread will be tightened to hold the cervix firmly closed for the remainder of the pregnancy. The thread will be removed at the thirty-seventh week of pregnancy, but it can be removed earlier in the pregnancy if a woman's water breaks or contractions start. Moreover, most women who need a cerclage in one pregnancy will need to have a cerclage placed in future pregnancies. Unfortunately, it is difficult to detect a weak cervix without knowledge of prior trauma (such as procedures to eliminate cervical dysplasia, cervical cancer, or previous second-trimester miscarriages).

A stillbirth is defined as a fetal death occurring after 20 weeks of pregnancy. Unlike miscarriage, which is found to be much more common, a stillbirth occurs in 1 out of 160 pregnancies (ACOG 2009). The most prevalent risk factors in women associated with this tragic event is being African American, being over the age of 35, no previous births, and having a BMI over 30. Other risk factors related to those listed above include chromosomal abnormalities affecting the fetus, multiple pregnancies, diabetes, hypertension, preeclampsia, syphilis, and smoking (McClure, Nalubamba-Phiri, & Goldenberg, 2006).

A SPERM'S JOURNEY FOR THAT "GOLDEN" EGG!

Given the amount of unintended pregnancies experienced in the United States every year, one may think that getting pregnant is a very easy task to undertake. After ejaculation, it can take 75 minutes for the sperm to reach the outer portion of the fallopian tubes (Gilbert & Harmon, 2002). That's pretty impressive, but many factors have to be in line for that one sperm to be successful in its mission. Any sperm making the journey into a woman's reproductive tract has a difficult road ahead!

When a man ejaculates into a woman's vagina (and remember that an ejaculation can carry anywhere from 200 to 500 million sperm), the sperm have to make it through the acidic environment of the vagina to the cervix (Jones & Lopez, 2006). Over 99 percent of sperm *do not* survive their journey through the vagina. Around 1 million sperm make it to the cervix from the vagina. At the cervix, the sperm can only hope a woman is close to ovulating or recently has, thus ensuring that their journey through the cervix will not be blocked by any cervical mucus. When ovulation occurs, the cervical mucus becomes more hospitable to sperm to improve chances of survival and ease of passage. Yet, unfortunately, the cervix also has numerous crevasses that sperm might find difficult to escape. From there, the 1,000 sperm that have survived the cervix now have to swim their way through the uterus. When the sperm reach the uterus, the uterus activates an upsurge of white blood cells (cells of the immune system involved in defending the body against both infectious disease and foreign materials). These cells begin to engulf any sperm that have not made their way to the fallopian tubes. Approximately 200 to 500 sperm make it to the fallopian tubes from

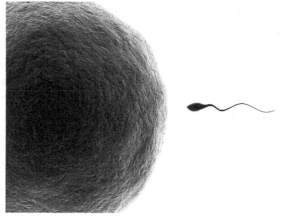

the uterus. Some swim to the fallopian tube that does not contain an oocyte, while around 20 to 200 make it to the egg (Jones & Lopez, 2006). So from a starting point of almost 200 to 500 million sperm, less than 1 percent will actually have a chance of fertilizing an egg—against all odds, though only one is needed!

The sperm and egg unite in one of the fallopian tubes to form a one-celled entity called a *zygote*. Fertilization (or conception) must take place near the fimbriae of the fallopian tube. The process of fertilization can take one to two days to occur. If fertilization is successful, the zygote will be pushed towards the uterus by the cilia of the fallopian tube. The zygote has 46 chromosomes—23 from the mother and 23 from the father. These chromosomes will help determine the fetus' sex and traits, such as eye and hair color. The zygote begins to divide rapidly forming a cluster of cells resembling a tiny raspberry as it journeys through the fallopian tube to the uterus (Jones & Lopez, 2006).

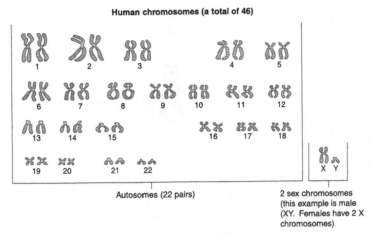

© 2011 by Blamb. Used under license of Shutterstock, Inc.

Six to seven days after fertilization, this new cell mass is around 100 cells and is called a *blastocyst*. The inner cell mass will become the embryo and the outer portion of cells will become the placenta, umbilical cord and amniotic sac. Implantation in the endometrial lining can only occur at this stage of development (Heffner & Schust, 2006). Time is of the essence! Depending on the length of a woman's menstrual cycle, she may only have days from bleeding. If the blastocyst does not burrow in the endometrial lining and "hijack" the woman's menstrual cycle, the fertilized egg will be sloughed off with the rest of the endometrium (Wilcox, Baird, & Weinberg, 1999). The woman will never know that a pregnancy was almost imminent.

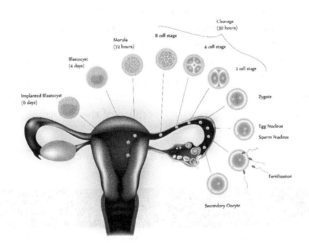

PLANNING A PREGNANCY

There is no reason why couples that want to get pregnant cannot plan the pregnancy to improve their chances of a healthy pregnancy and birth outcome. If a couple is seriously contemplating being parents, then what can they do besides participate in unprotected coitus? First of all, the couple should discuss when they want to have the baby born. If it is September and they were hoping for a May baby, well, that's not going to happen. A couple should begin planning a pregnancy a year *before* the planned birth.

A woman needs to stop any hormonal method that was preventing her from getting pregnant at least three months before initiating unprotected coitus. One reason is to give her body enough time to orchestrate a menstrual cycle of its own to help determine the days a woman is close to ovulating.

Also, women need to consider taking a prenatal vitamin daily at least three months before participating in unprotected coitus. Why? Well, when do women usually find out they are pregnant? If they were planning the pregnancy, it might be weeks into it, if it was unintended, they might not realize (or be in denial) that they are pregnant until months into it. Taking prenatal vitamins before a pregnancy helps to ensure that when a woman does find out she is preg-

© 2011 by karen roach. Used under license of Shutterstock, Inc.

nant, the embryo or fetus has been receiving the nutrients needed from the mother. Moreover, folic acid taken before pregnancy and for the first three months of pregnancy can reduce the risk of neural tube defects (Mosley et al., 2009).

HORMONAL SURGE

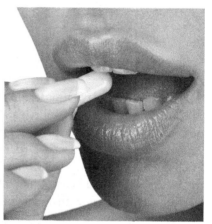

© 2011 by Yuri Arcurs. Used under license of Shutterstock, Inc.

After ovulation, the corpus luteum (the disintegrating follicle that contained the ovum) increases the production of estrogen and progesterone to help maintain a receptive uterine lining for the expected blastocyst (Gilbert & Harmon, 2002). When a pregnancy is established (meaning the blastocyst has burrowed itself in the uterine lining), the woman's body begins producing large quantities of estrogen, progesterone, and human chorionic gonadotropin (hCG) to help the pregnancy continue. Pregnant women will make more estrogen in nine months than a woman who never is pregnant will make in her whole entire lifetime! Pregnant women will also produce eight times the amount of progesterone that non-pregnant women produce (Bonillas & Feehan, 2008). Review Table 9.1 for changes that can occur during a pregnancy because of these hormones.

TABLE 9.1: Internal and External Physical Changes during Pregnancy

FIRST TRIMESTER (WEEKS 1 THROUGH 13)	EXPLANATION FOR CHANGE
1.1 Missed period	Hormones secreted by the blastocyst (after burrowing into the endometrial lining) take control of the menstrual cycle.
1.2 Nausea & vomiting	Due to rapidly increasing levels of the hormone, human chorionic gonadotropin (hCG). Nausea tends to peak around the same time as levels of hCG.
1.3 Sensitivity to odors	Due to high levels of the hormone, estrogen.
1.4 Fatigue	Occurs due to higher levels of the hormone, progesterone, in order for the body to focus its energy on sustaining the pregnancy.

FIRST TRIMESTER (Continued) (WEEKS 1 THROUGH 13)		EXPLANATION FOR CHANGE
1.5	Breast enlargement	Due to increased levels of estrogen, the mammary glands begin to enlarge in preparation for breastfeeding.
1.6	Breast tenderness	The enlargement of the mammary glands make the breasts become tender.
1.7	Darkening of the areola	The pigmented areas around each breast's nipple darkens due to increased levels of progesterone and estrogen (and believed to help the newborn find the breast at birth).
1.8	Areola increases in size	Due to increased hormone levels (and believed to help the newborn find the breast at birth).
1.9	Mood swings	Partly due to surges in hormones–characterized by change in emotional stability and irritability.
1.10	Expanding uterus	The placenta produces progesterone, which relaxes the muscles of the uterus (womb) so they can stretch as the pregnancy progresses.

SECOND TRIMESTER (WEEKS 14 THROUGH 27)		EXPLANATION FOR CHANGE
2.1	Slower digestion	High levels of progesterone slow down the contractions of the esophagus and intestine, thus slowing down digestion.
2.2	Constipation	Due to a slower digestion.
2.3	Hemorrhoids	Due to constipation.
2.4	Heartburn	The placenta produces progesterone, which relaxes the valve that separates the esophagus from the stomach, allowing gastric acids to seep back up, causing an unpleasant burning sensation.
2.5	Backaches	Due to the expanding uterus affecting posture.
2.6	Pinching of sciatic nerve	Nerve in the hip/buttock area gets pinched because of pressure exerted on it by the expanding uterus.
2.7	Facial skin changes	Dark patches appear on the face due to hormonal changes.
2.8	Increased frequency in urination	Due to increased blood flow to the kidneys and pressure from the weight of the pregnancy on the bladder.
2.9	Edema	Swelling of the ankles, hands and face due to fluid retention.
2.10	Expanding uterus	Due to progesterone, which in turn relaxes the muscles of the uterus so they can stretch as the pregnancy progresses.
2.11	Abdominal enlargement	Due to the progression of the pregnancy, the uterus expands into the abdominal cavity.
2.12	Increase in blood volume	Due to the need for extra blood flow to the uterus.
2.13	Heart growth	Due to the body needing to supply more blood for the growing fetus and placenta.
2.14	Quickening	Feeling fetal movements for the first time.

(continued)

SECOND TRIMESTER (Continued) (WEEKS 14 THROUGH 27)	EXPLANATION FOR CHANGE
2.15 Stretch marks	Due to the expanding abdomen, breasts, legs, buttocks. Stretch marks occur when the dermis, the middle layer of your skin, is stretched to a point where its elasticity begins to break down.
2.16 Sweating	Due to hormonal changes, increased effort on physical activities due to the expanding uterus and the fetus begins to radiate body heat.
2.17 Difficulty in sleeping	Due to fetal movements or frequent urination at night.
2.18 Leukorrhea	Higher levels of estrogen increase blood flow to the vagina, which, in turn, increases the release of a white-colored odorless vaginal discharge (sign of a healthy vagina).
2.19 Hair Growth	Due to hormone stimulation of hair follicles on the heard, arms, legs and face.
2.20 Dry, itchy skin	Particularly on the abdomen as the skin continues to grow and stretch due to the expanding uterus.
2.21 "Linea Nigra"	A dark line running from the pubic bone up the center of the abdomen to the ribs, which is caused by the increase in hormones.

THIRD TRIMESTER (WEEKS 28 THROUGH 40)	EXPLANATION FOR CHANGE
3.1 Heart turns on its side	Takes place in order to make room for expanding uterus, which pushes other organs up as well.
3.2 Varicose veins	Swollen/bluish veins that may bulge near the surface of the skin, usually behind the legs. As the uterus grows, it puts pressure on the large vein on the right side of the body, which in turn increases pressure on the veins in the legs, making the veins swell from the extra pressure to return the blood from the extremities to the heart (as they work against gravity).
3.3 Heartburn	The growing fetus crowds the abdominal cavity, pushing the stomach acids back up into the esophagus.
3.4 Hemorrhoids	Due to constipation.
3.5 Leg cramps	Believed to be due to lack of calcium in the body.
3.6 Shortness of breath	Due to the expanding uterus pushing up against the diaphragm.
3.7 Braxton-Hicks	Usually painless uterine contractions that help the uterus prepare contractions for labor.
3.8 Increased frequency in urination	Due to increased blood flow to the kidneys and pressure from the weight of the pregnancy on the bladder.
3.9 Stretch marks	Due to the expanding abdomen, breasts, thighs, and buttocks.
3.10 Dry, itchy skin	Particularly on the abdomen as the skin continues to grow and stretch due to the expanding uterus.
3.11 Naval protrusion	Belly-button sticking out is due to the expanding abdominal cavity.

THIRD TRIMESTER (Continued) (WEEKS 28 THROUGH 40)	EXPLANATION FOR CHANGE
3.12 Colostrum	Yellow, watery fluid produced by the mammary glands. Colostrum contains large amounts of antibodies that help protect the mucous membranes in the throat, lungs, and intestines of the infant. White blood cells are also present in large numbers and begin protecting the infant from harmful bacteria and viruses. Beneficial bacteria are also established in the digestive tract of an infant when colostrum is ingested.
3.13 Estrogen	A pregnant woman will have more estrogen in her body during the nine months of pregnancy than a woman who never gets pregnant will have in her entire lifetime.
3.14 Progesterone	By the end of the pregnancy, levels of this hormone will increase seven times its normal levels during pregnancy.

Source: Bonillas, C., & Feehan, R. (2008). Tools for teaching: Normalizing the changes experienced during each trimester of pregnancy. *The Journal of Perinatal Education, 17*, 39–43.

CALCULATING A DUE DATE

The medical community counts the duration of a pregnancy beginning from the last menstruation to 40 weeks in the future. At that last menstrual period, the woman hadn't even participated in coitus that resulted in fertilization. Depending on the length of a woman's menstrual cycle, the dating of a pregnancy is measured beginning one to three weeks before ovulation. This practice, though, is convenient because it is easy to determine when the last menstrual period was, while both fertilization and implantation can only be hypothesized.

TRIMESTERS

© 2011 by Monkey Business. Used under license of Shutterstock, Inc.

According to the American Congress of Obstetricians and Gynecologists (ACOG, 2010), the 40 weeks (around 280 days) of pregnancy are divided into three trimesters. Each trimester lasts about 12 to 13 weeks each (or about 3 months). The first trimester is considered weeks 0 to 13 (or months 1 to 3), the second trimester is weeks 14 to 27 (or months 4 to 6), and the third trimester is deemed to be weeks 28 to 40 (or months 7 to 9).

FIRST TRIMESTER

Finding out you or your partner is pregnant is always a surprise, even if the pregnancy was planned! As exciting as being pregnant (or having a partner who's pregnant) will be, it is strongly recommended that a pregnancy be kept a secret during the first trimester.

Losing a pregnancy during the first three months of pregnancy is very likely, regardless of the health of the woman (Gilbert & Harmon, 2002). Because of this, it is best to wait until the fourteenth week of pregnancy to let everyone in on the wonderful surprise.

Most women will not see a difference in the size of their abdomen at this time, but they might with their breast size! Many women will experience certain symptoms that imply a pregnancy has occurred. Most obvious is that every pregnant woman will stop menstruating. Hormonal changes during pregnancy cease the endometrial lining from growing. Moreover, the cervix creates a mucous plug that prevents passage to the uterus. Thus, withdrawal bleeding similar to menstruation is not possible during pregnancy. If a woman is bleeding, that might indicate bleeding from the vagina or cervix, but endometrial bleeding is rare (Gilbert & Harmon, 2002). Around 80 percent of women will experience nausea and/or vomiting. This is a good thing! For most women, the nausea and/or vomiting are side effects to the upsurge in certain hormones that are helping sustain the pregnancy. Review Table 9.1 for a list of the internal and external physical changes women may experience during pregnancy (Bonillas & Feehan, 2008).

Embryo Development The embryonic period begins around three weeks after conception occurred and lasts until around the ninth week of gestation. The placenta has not fully developed during this stage. The embryo creates a yolk sac that provides nourishment until the placenta is capable of that responsibility. The embryo's brain, spinal cord, heart, and other organs begin to form during the first trimester. At the gestational age of three weeks, the embryo is around the size of the tip of a pen! Five weeks after conception, the embryo is a little bigger than the top of a pencil eraser. By the end of this stage, the embryo is now a whopping half-inch long!

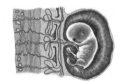

© 2011 by EmeCeDesigns. Used under license of Shutterstock, Inc.

SECOND TRIMESTER

Don't be shy about sharing the great news with anyone and everyone! Of course, some people probably already may have suspected something, especially if the woman was running to the bathroom all the time (to vomit or to urinate) or craving uncommon foods, such as liver (which probably meant she was low in iron). A woman's abdomen will start to protrude during this trimester for the majority of women. That means most of her clothes will start feeling tight. By 14 to 16 weeks into the pregnancy, the placenta assumes the responsibility for maintenance of the pregnancy by delivering oxygen, nutrients, and producing the necessary hormones (Gilbert & Harmon, 2002). Along with estrogen, progesterone, and hCG, the placenta also produces human placental lactogen (hPL). This hormone helps break down fats in the pregnant women to provide fuel to the developing fetus. Elevated levels of this hormone may lead to insulin resistance and carbohydrate intolerance in the pregnant woman, which increases the risk of gestational diabetes mellitus (GDM). As will be discussed later in this chapter, healthy eating habits (i.e., eating nutrient-dense foods over calorie-dense/low nutrient-dense foods) throughout the pregnancy help provide the fetus and the mother with the needed nutrients.

Fetal Development At this stage, the fetus has functioning organs, nerves, and muscles. Tissue that will become bone develops around the fetal head and within the arms and legs. Fat begins to accumulate under the skin around the seventeenth week. Around the twenty-fourth week, the uterus and ovaries are in place in a female fetus. The ovaries are filled with 5 million immature ovarian follicles (Jones & Lopez, 2006). For a male fetus, the testes are beginning to descend from the abdomen to the outside of the body. By the end of the second trimester, the fetus will be around nine inches long and weigh nearly two pounds.

THIRD TRIMESTER

During the last three months of the pregnancy it will be hard to deny that a woman is pregnant! There are women, though, especially if they are obese, that do not "show" at all. By the end of the pregnancy, the uterus will have expanded around 40 inches! As it expanded, it moved a woman's organs out of the way to make room for itself. The uterus doesn't actually grow. The uterus stretches to accompany the growing fetus, placenta, and amniotic fluid. For many women, their breasts increased at least one cup size during the pregnancy. Their shoe size will also increase, as will the width of their feet. Fluid retention is normal in the hands and feet, but if it is felt suddenly (instead of a gradual increase over days or weeks) then this might warrant a call to the doctor to confirm it is not preeclampsia (a medical condition in which high blood pressure arises in pregnancy).

Many couples prepare for the upcoming arrival of their baby by participating in birthing classes, touring the hospital or birthing center where they will deliver, packing a bag for the mother and baby, having an infant car seat if leaving the hospital or birthing center by car (the medical staff will not let you take a baby in a car without an infant car seat), and having a room or at least a crib waiting for the baby's homecoming.

Fetal Development At this stage, the fetus is busy gaining weight—about ½ a pound a week during the last month. The lungs are the last organ to develop. From 38 to 40 weeks gestation, the fetus is around 14 inches long and weighs about 7½ pounds.

LABOR AND BIRTH

The majority of women do not deliver on their due date (only around 10 percent do). If labor is not induced for any reason, most women give birth between a timeframe of 2 weeks before or 2 weeks after their due date. A woman delivering "at term" is defined giving birth between 37 to 42 weeks gestation. Most women are not allowed to carry a pregnancy past 42 weeks because the placenta starts disintegrating, which places the fetus at greater risk of death (ACOG, 2010). A premature delivery is giving birth before 37 weeks gestation.

FIRST STAGE OF LABOR

This stage begins when uterine contractions are consistent and can be timed every 5 to 20 minutes. The purpose of these contractions is not to push the baby out but to open the cervix to allow the woman to push the baby out during the second stage of labor. Levels of oxytocin and prostaglandins increase in women during labor. Oxytocin has been found to improve the ability of the uterus to contract during labor, and prostaglandins help the cervix become softer and shorter (Gilbert & Harmon, 2002). Many women describe the contractions as menstrual cramps that will progressively increase in intensity and duration. This stage ends when the cervix is completely effaced (i.e., thinned out) and dilated (i.e., opened up) to 10 centimeters (cm). This stage is the longest stage and is broken down into three phases.

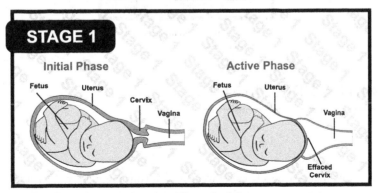

© 2011 by udiax. Used under license of Shutterstock, Inc.

The early labor phase begins at the onset of labor until the cervix is effaced and dilated to 3 cm. The active labor phase continues until the cervix is 100 percent effaced (completely thinned out) and 7 cm dilated. It is during the active labor phase that women can request pain relievers, such as an epidural. During this stage, the mucous plug dislodges and the amniotic sac may rupture. On average, the first stage of labor lasts around 10 to 16 hours. Just as every pregnancy can be experienced differently, so can every labor. Some women end this stage after 3 hours, whereas other women take 24 hours or more. The transition phase continues until the cervix is fully dilated to 10 cm (around 4 inches).

SECOND STAGE OF LABOR

This stage begins when the cervix has dilated to 10 cm and it's time for the mother to push. On average, the second stage of labor lasts around 30 minutes to 2 hours. This stage ends at the delivery of the baby.

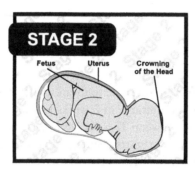

© 2011 by udiax. Used under license of Shutterstock, Inc.

THIRD STAGE OF LABOR

This stage begins when the baby has been delivered. On average, the third and final stage of labor occurs up to 30 minutes after birth. This stage ends at the delivery of the placenta.

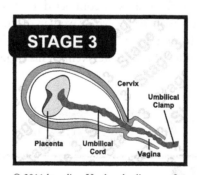

© 2011 by udiax. Used under license of Shutterstock, Inc.

HAVING A HEALTHY PREGNANCY

PRENATAL NUTRITION

One of the few times that a woman purposely gains weight is during pregnancy (O'Toole, Sawicki & Artal, 2003). Extra energy is required during pregnancy for the growth and maintenance of the fetus, placenta, and maternal tissue (IOM, 1990; Rasmussen & Yaktine, 2009). The fetus is a continuous feeder, whereas the mother is a periodic feeder (Gilbert & Harmon, 2002). A woman's dietary intake during pregnancy affects fetal growth and development. But just because a woman is gaining gestational weight does not mean she is providing the nutrients needed by her body and the fetus to achieve an optimal birth weight and pregnancy outcome (Stotland et al., 2005).

© 2011 by Otna Ydur. Used under license of Shutterstock, Inc.

© 2011 by Samuel Borges. Used under license of Shutterstock, Inc.

Seiga-Riz and her colleagues (2002) found that pregnant women were more likely to compromise their nutrient intake by drinking soft drinks over more nutrient-dense beverages, such as milk. High fat diets, specifically high-fat animal products, were also very common. These finding follow the trend in expansion of fast-food restaurants both in number and in nontraditional locations such as gasoline stations, department stores and even hospitals (Morland, Wing, & Diez, 2002). The traditional menus (e.g., soft drink, French fries, and hamburgers) are high in fat and low in nutrient density, which increase the risk of obesity, particularly with the trend in supersizing these low-cost meals. Diets high in fat and empty calories need to be of concern for pregnant women given a tendency to gain weight above the weight gain recommendation and lack of nutrient-dense foods needed to achieve a healthy pregnancy (Davis et al., 2009).

PHYSICAL ACTIVITY DURING PREGNANCY

In 2002, ACOG concluded that exercise during pregnancy may provide additional health benefits to women. The ACOG guidelines for exercise during pregnancy state that "in the absence of either medical or obstetric complications, 30 minutes or more of moderate exercise a day on most, if not all, days of the week is recommended for pregnant women" (page 171). Recommended prenatal exercises include swimming, walking and yoga (American College of Sports Medicine, 2000).

WEIGHT GAIN DURING PREGNANCY

© 2011 by Ken Hurst. Used under license of Shutterstock, Inc.

In 1990, the Institute of Medicine (IOM) issued guidelines for weight gain during pregnancy (IOM, 1990). These guidelines have recently been revised because of changing weight patterns among women in the United States and because the 1990 pregnancy guidelines did not offer specific advice for obese women (Rasmussen & Yaktine, 2009). A woman with a normal body mass index (BMI) of 18.5 to 24.9 is recommended to gain between 25 to 35 pounds during a pregnancy. A woman considered overweight (BMI of 25.0 to 29.9) is advised to gain between 15 to 25 pounds during a pregnancy. An obese woman (BMI ≥30.0) is counseled to limit her gestational weight gain to 11 to 20 pounds (Rasmussen & Yaktine, 2009).

Where is this extra weight going? According to the March of Dimes, Table 9.2 provides a description of how the weight is distributed. Women vary, though, in how much they gain and where that extra weight ends up, especially with the size of the baby and how much extra fat they've gained during the pregnancy.

The average BMI is increasing among all age categories, and women are entering pregnancy at higher weights (Ogden et al., 2006; Siega-Riz, Siega-Riz & Laraia, 2006). Currently, one in five women is obese at the beginning of pregnancy (Kim et al., 2007). Moreover, overweight and obese women are more likely to gain excessive weight during their pregnancy and are less likely to lose it after delivery (Olson et al., 2003).

© 2011 by Andrey Bandurenko. Used under license of Shutterstock, Inc.

© 2011 by Poulsons Photography. Used under license of Shutterstock, Inc.

Maternal obesity during pregnancy has been connected to such complications as cesarean delivery (Myles, Gooch & Santolaya, 2002), gestational hypertension (Yogev & Visser, 2009), preeclampsia (Robinson et al. 2005), GDM (Rosenn 2008), and macrosomia (Murphy et al. 2008). Obesity during pregnancy is also associated with greater use of health care services and longer hospital stay (Chu et al., 2008). Interestingly, a recent study found that more than half of all obstetricians consider their training on weight management as inadequate or non-existent (Power, Cogswell, & Schulkin, 2006).

TABLE 9.2: Gestational Weight Gain

Baby	7½ pounds
Fat and proteins	7 pounds
Retained water	4 pounds
Blood	3 pounds
Amniotic fluid	2 pounds
Breasts	2 pounds
Uterus	2 pounds
Placenta	1½ pounds
TOTAL	29 pounds

Reproduced by permission of the March of Dimes. Copyright 2011.

PREGNANCY COMPLICATIONS

INFERTILITY

Infertility can be defined as having unprotected coitus for one year without becoming pregnant. Thirty-five percent of fertility problems reside with the woman, 35 percent with the man, 20 percent with both partners, and 10 percent of the time, the cause is unknown (Jones & Lopez, 2006). The leading cause of infertility in females is the failure to ovulate. The leading cause of infertility in males is a low sperm count. According to the American Fertility Association, sperm count has to be lower than 20 million per ejaculate to be considered low.

Even though the majority of births (99.8 percent) occur to women under 45 years of age (Martin et al., 2009), age is known to affect fertility for both women and men. A woman's fertility peaks around 20 to 24 (Crooks & Baur, 2011). Fecundity begins to wane around the age of 30, with a dramatic fall for women over the age of 35 (Spandorfer et al., 1998). A woman in her late twenties does not produce as much progesterone as she did when she was younger. The number and quality of ovarian follicles also diminishes. This causes a decline in estrogen production and ovulation does not occur on a monthly basis, making conception more difficult (Harvard Medical School, 2005).

According to the American Society for Reproductive Medicine, cigarette smoking is harmful to a woman's ovaries, and the degree of harm is dependent on how much and how long a woman smokes. Smoking appears to accelerate the loss of oocytes and may advance the time of menopause by several years. Moreover, components in cigarette smoke have been shown to interfere with the ability of cells in the ovary to make estrogen and to cause a woman's eggs to be more prone to genetic abnormalities.

Men's fertility can also be affected by smoking. Smoking can decrease sperm motility and increase the number of structurally abnormal sperm in ejaculated semen. If realizing the dangers of smoking to one's heart or lungs isn't enough to help people stop smoking, maybe acknowledging the link between infertility and smoking will!

ECTOPIC PREGNANCY

An ectopic pregnancy occurs when the embryo grows outside of the uterus. This usually takes place in one of the fallopian tubes, but can also take place on an ovary, cervix, or somewhere else in the pelvic cavity (Jones & Lopez, 2006). This is a life-threatening situation, and immediate medical attention is needed. Women at risk for an ectopic pregnancy have a history of reproductive tract infections (Cottrell, 2010; Honey & Templeton, 2002), are smokers (Roelands et al., 2009), or have undergone fertility treatment (Chang & Suh, 2010).

MULTIPLE PREGNANCIES

Carrying twins occurs in 1 of every 85 pregnancies. Dizygotic (or fraternal) twins occur when two ova are released and each is fertilized by a different sperm (Jones & Lopez, 2006). The incidence of fraternal twins is genetic and influenced by race and inherited factors from the mother, but not the father. Around the world, African-American women have the highest rate of fraternal twins, whereas Japanese women have the lowest rate. Monozygotic (or identical) twins are rarer than fraternal twins and occur when a zygote divides into two. Carrying a pregnancy with identical twins is not genetic and, thus, is not influenced by race, inheritance, or the mother's age.

© 2011 by Paul Matthew Photography. Used under license of Shutterstock, Inc.

Women who use assisted reproductive technology to get pregnant increase their chances of carrying multiple pregnancies (Jones & Lopez, 2006). Given the recent publicized accounts of women carrying sextuplets or more, the Society for Assisted Reproductive Technology has reported that multiple pregnancies carrying triplets has decreased to almost 2 percent of women under the age of 35 in 2007. In 2003, that number was 6.4 percent. As more clinicians transfer no more than two embryos into a woman's uterus, the likelihood that a woman will carry a pregnancy with more than one fetus decreases. Multiple pregnancies and pregnancies assisted by reproductive technology are much more likely to end before term and have babies born at low or very low birth weight (Kogan et al., 2000).

GESTATIONAL DIABETES MELLITUS (GDM)

GDM is considered the most common medical complication of pregnancy (Baptiste-Roberts et al., 2009). GDM can be defined as glucose intolerance with an onset or first recognition occurring during pregnancy (American Diabetes Association, 2004). The risk of developing GDM is about two and four times higher among overweight and obese women, respectively, when compared with normal-weight pregnant women (Chu et al., 2007). In a recent study, Zhang and her colleagues (2006) found that women who lived a sedentary lifestyle had a higher risk of GDM than women who were physically active before and during their pregnancy. GDM increases the risk of developing type-2 diabetes not only for the mother, but for the baby as well (Baptiste-Roberts et al., 2009).

POSTPARTUM HEALTH

POSTPARTUM BLEEDING

After a birth, a woman will bleed anywhere from four to six weeks. This is not the time to wear tampons, but a time to make sure she has a good supply of menstrual pads for many heavy days. This should not be considered a normal menstrual period. This postpartum bleeding and discharge is called lochia. The bleeding occurs for so long because the detached placenta has left a wound on the uterine lining. This area has to heal, and part of that healing is bleeding. The bleeding is not an indication that a woman cannot become pregnant at this time. It is recommended that women in heterosexual relationships wait at least six weeks postpartum to participate in coitus. But that timeframe should also adhere to when the woman is ready to resume vaginal/penile intercourse (which could be longer than six weeks). As the uterus heals, the vaginal discharge will change from a bright red, to a pink, to a yellow. By the time a woman attends her six-week postpartum visit, the lochia should be yellow or ceased completely. This postpartum visit is needed so the obstetrician or midwife can check on the woman's physical recovery from pregnancy and delivery, see how she's doing emotionally, and address any needs. This is also a good time to speak with the clinician about contraceptive options so an unplanned pregnancy doesn't occur, especially so soon after giving birth.

POSTPARTUM DEPRESSION (PPD)

According to Postpartum Support International, while many women experience some mild mood changes during or after the birth of a child, 15 to 20 percent of women experience more significant symptoms of depression or anxiety. One cause for this is the sharp and rapid drop in estrogen and progesterone soon after giving birth. A number of hormones, including estrogen and progesterone, directly affect the brain chemistry that controls emotions and mood (Bloch, 2003).

© 2011 by Golden Pixels LLC. Used under license of Shutterstock, Inc.

A woman with PPD might experience feelings of anger, sadness, irritability, guilt, lack of interest in the baby, changes in eating and sleeping habits, trouble concentrating, thoughts of hopelessness and sometimes even thoughts of harming the baby or herself. This is a serious condition that should not be taken lightly. With medication and/or therapy, the majority of women recover from PPD.

"BREAST IS BEST"

Breastfeeding is recommended as the preferred method of infant feeding for the first year of life or longer and exclusive breastfeeding is recommended for the first six months of life (Gartner et al., 2005). Figure 9.1 illustrates the percentage of infants that are breastfed at six months of age in the United States. How does your state measure up? The majority of American infants are breastfed at birth (over 70 percent in 2007), but we lag behind in breastfeeding our infants at three or six months of age. Why do you think that's the case? And why do European countries have better breastfeeding rates than the United States? According to the National Centers for Health Statistics (McDowell et al., 2008), Mexican-American women, regardless of income and age, are more likely to breastfeed in this country. Even though the rate of breastfeeding in the African-American community has improved in the past decade, they remain the least likely to breastfeed.

© 2011 by Valua Vitaly. Used under license of Shutterstock, Inc.

© 2011 by OLJ Studio. Used under license of Shutterstock, Inc.

There are a number of health benefits to the mother if she breastfeeds. These benefits include decreased postpartum bleeding and more rapid uterine involution (the uterus shrinks back to size) attributable to the increased concentrations of oxytocin (Chua et al., 1994). Breastfeeding mothers have been found to return to their pre-pregnancy weight earlier than women who do not breastfeed (Dewey, Heinig, & Nommsen, 1993). Moreover, longer duration of breastfeeding has been associated with lower maternal weight gain 10 to 15 years later (Gunderson, 2007). Also, breastfeeding has been found to reduce the risk of breast (Collaborative Group on Hormonal Factors in Breast Cancer, 2002) and ovarian cancer (Jernstrom et al., 2004).

The American Academy of Pediatrics (2005) urges breastfeeding mothers to avoid the use of alcoholic beverages because alcohol is concentrated in breast milk and its use can inhibit milk production. An occasional celebratory single, small alcoholic drink is acceptable, but breastfeeding should be avoided for two hours after the drink (Anderson, 1995).

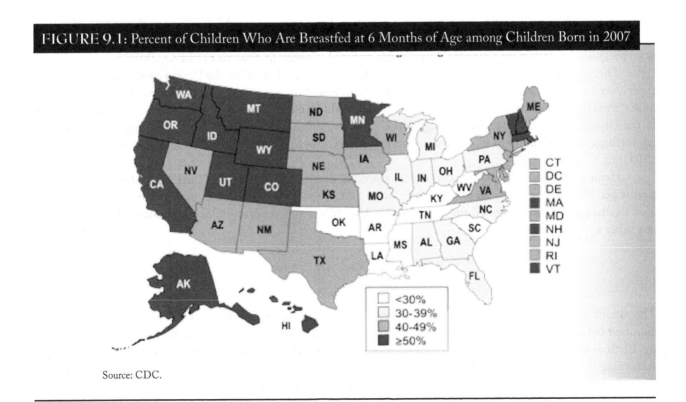

FIGURE 9.1: Percent of Children Who Are Breastfed at 6 Months of Age among Children Born in 2007

Source: CDC.

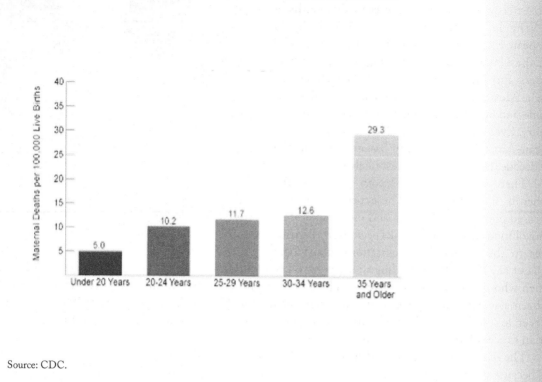

Source: CDC.

MATERNAL MORTALITY

Maternal mortality can be defined as the death of a woman during pregnancy, childbirth, or in the first 42 days after delivery (Hogan et al., 2010). Around the world, the country of Niger has the highest lifetime risk of women dying from pregnancy-related complications (1 in 7). Ireland has the lowest lifetime risk (1 in 48,000).

The lifetime risk in the United States is one in 4,800. From 1980 to 2008, the United States and Canada have experienced a 33 percent increase in the maternal mortality rate (Hogan et al., 2010). Forty nations have a lower risk of maternal death than here in the United States (The World Bank, 2007). The top three causes of maternal death in the United States are preeclampsia (high blood pressure), eclampsia (convulsions or seizures), and postpartum hemorrhage (severe bleeding). Postpartum hemorrhage is the leading cause of maternal death around the world (McCormick et al., 2002).

Healthy People 2020 has a target of 11.4 maternal deaths per 100,000 live births. In 2007, 12.7 maternal deaths per 100,000 live births occurred in the United States. For African American women, though, the ratio was 36.5 deaths per 100,000 births (Kung et al., 2008). Also, women 35 years and older were more likely to die than any other age group (see Figure 9.2).

INFANT MORTALITY

The rate of infant mortality is used to indicate how healthy a country is. Infant mortality is defined as a death of an infant before her or his first birthday. In 2005, the United States ranked thirtieth in the world in infant mortality. Birth defects are the leading cause of infant mortality in the United States (Mathews & MacDorman, 2010). According to the Centers for Health Statistics (Mathews & MacDorman, 2010), infant mortality rates were higher for male infants, African-American babies, babies that were part of a multiple pregnancy, and babies born preterm (before 37 weeks gestation) or at low birth weight (below 5½ pounds).

One in eight births in the United States is born premature. The lower the gestational age, the more likely that baby will not survive. Babies with a birth defect are also more likely to be born premature and are at risk of dying even if the birth defect is not life-threatening (Callaghan et al., 2006). As women age, they are more likely to deliver a baby with chromosomal abnormalities. Moreover, birth defects have also been found in babies whose fathers are at an advanced paternal age (Zhu et al., 2005).

REFLECTIONS

The United States is considered one of the wealthiest and most powerful countries in the world. Yet we have one of the highest rates of abortion when compared to other developed countries. Why do you think that is the case? Religion strongly influences politics in this country. Why do you think religion affects public policy here in the United States more so than in other developed countries?

We also have very low rates of breastfeeding and high rates of c-sections. We have the best medical technology *in the world*, yet our mothers and babies die at an alarming rate. Ironically, more women and infants would die annually if we didn't have the medical facilities we do have. What do you think is needed to improve our country's maternal and infant health?

CRITICAL THINKING SKILL

Level 4, Analysis. Examine and break information into parts by identifying motives or cause. Make inferences and find evidence to support generalizations.

Bloom's Taxonomy Key Words. Compare and contrast, list, relationships, examine, distinguish, predict, breakdown, outline, and analyze.

CRITICAL THINKING QUESTIONS

1. A friend has confided in you that she's pregnant and she's asking for your advice. Would your advice differ if your friend was 15 years old rather than 35? How about if she was married versus single? Already had four children? Almost died during her last pregnancy? Why or why not?
2. Do you think if we decreased the rate of unintended pregnancies in the United States, we would indirectly lower the rate of abortion as well? Why or why not?
3. Why is it that a disproportionate amount of women of color and in poverty terminate a pregnancy?
4. How do you think public policy has hindered women's ability to prevent unintended pregnancies?

WEBSITES

www.acog.org
The American Congress of Obstetricians and Gynecologists

www.americanpregnancy.org
The American Pregnancy Association

www.asrm.org

The American Society for Reproductive Medicine

www.marchofdimes.com

The March of Dimes

www.cdc.gov/nchs

The National Center for Health Statistics

www.postpartum.net

Postpartum Support International

www.sart.org

Society for Assisted Reproductive Technology

REFERENCES

American Academy of Pediatrics. (2005). *Policy statement: Breastfeeding and the use of human milk.* Washington, D.C.: AAP.

American College of Sports Medicine (2000). *ACSM's guidelines for exercise, testing and prescription,* 6th ed. Philadelphia, PA: Lippincott, Williams, & Wilkins.

American College of Obstetricians and Gynecologists. (2009). *Evaluation of stillbirths and neonatal deaths. ACOG committee opinion, 383.* Washington, D.C.: ACOG.

American Congress of Obstetricians and Gynecologists. (2010). *How your baby grows during pregnancy.* Washington, D.C.: ACOG.

American Congress of Obstetricians and Gynecologists. (2002). Exercise during pregnancy and the postpartum period. ACOG committee opinion 267. *Obstetrics & Gynecology, 99,* 171–173.

American Congress of Obstetricians and Gynecologists (2001). Management of recurrent early pregnancy loss. *ACOG Practice Bulletin 24.*

American Diabetes Association. (2004). Gestational diabetes mellitus (position statement). *Diabetes Care, 27,* s88–s90.

Anderson, P. O. (1995). Alcohol and breastfeeding. *Journal of Human Lactation,* 11, 321–323.

Baptiste-Roberts, K., Barone, B., Gary, T., Golden, S., Wilson, L., Bass, E., & Nicholson, W. (2009). Risk factors for type 2 diabetes among women with gestational diabetes: A systematic review. *The American Journal of Medicine, 122,* 207–214.

Bloch, M. (2003). Endocrine factors in the etiology of postpartum depression. *Comprehensive Psychiatry, 44*(3) 234–246.

Bonillas, C., & Feehan, R. (2008). Tools for teaching: Normalizing the changes experienced during each trimester of pregnancy. *The Journal of Perinatal Education, 17,* 39-43.

Brown, L. (2007). Elevated risks of pregnancy complications and adverse outcomes with increasing maternal age. *Human Reproduction, 22*(5), 1264-1272.

Callaghan, W., MacDorman, M., Rasmussen, S., Qin C., & Lackritz, E. (2006). The contribution of preterm birth to infant mortality rates in the United States. *Pediatrics, 118,* 1566–1573.

Chang, H., & Suh, C. (2010). Ectopic pregnancy after assisted reproductive technology: What are the risk factors? *Current Opinion in Obstetrics & Gynecology, 22*(3), 202–207.

Chu, S., Bachman, D., Callaghan, W., Whitlock, E., Dietz, P., Berg, C., O'Keeffe-Rosetti, M., Bruce, F., & Hornbrook, M. (2008). Association between obesity during pregnancy and increased use of health care. *The New England Journal of Medicine, 358*, 1444–1453.

Chu, S. Callaghan, W., Kim, S., Schmid, C., Lau, J., England, L., & Dietz, P. (2007). Maternal obesity and risk of gestational diabetes mellitus. *Diabetes Care, 30*, 2070–2076.

Chua, S., Arulkumaran, S., Lim, I., Selamat, N., & Ratnam, S. (1994). Influence of breastfeeding and nipple stimulation on postpartum uterine activity. *British Journal of Obstetrics & Gynaecology, 101*, 804–805.

Cohen, S. (2006). Toward making abortion 'rare': The shifting battleground over the means to an end. *Guttmacher Policy Review, 9*(1), 1–5.

Collaborative Group on Hormonal Factors in Breast Cancer. (2002). Breast cancer and breastfeeding: Collaborative reanalysis of individual data from 47 epidemiological studies in 30 countries, including 50,302 women with breast cancer and 96,973 women without the disease. *Lancet, 360*, 187–195.

Cottrell, B. (2010). An updated review of evidence to discourage douching. *The American Journal of Maternal Child Nursing, 35*(2), 102–109.

Crooks, R., & Baur, K. (2011). *Our sexuality*, 11th ed. Belmont, CA: Wadsworth/Cengage Learning.

Davis, E. M., Zyzanski, S. J., Olson, C. M., Stange, K. C., & Horwitz, R. I. (2009). Racial, ethnic, and socioeconomic differences in the incidence of obesity related to childbirth. *American Journal of Public Health, 99*, 294–299.

Dewey, K., Heinig, M., & Nommsen, L. (1993). Maternal weight-loss patterns during prolonged lactation. *American Journal of Clinical Nutrition, 58*, 162–166.

Finer, L. B., & Henshaw, S. K., (2006). Disparities in rates of unintended pregnancy in the United States, 1994 and 2001. *Perspectives on Sexual and Reproductive Health, 38*, 90–96.

Gartner, L. M., Morton, J., Lawrence, R. A., Naylor, A. J., O'Hare, D., Schanler, R. J., & Eidelman, A. L. (2005). Breastfeeding and the use of human milk. *Pediatrics, 115*, 496–506.

Gilbert, E., & Harmon, J. (2002). *Manual of high risk pregnancy and delivery*, 3rd ed. St. Louis, MI: Mosby.

Gunderson, E. P. (2007). Breastfeeding after gestational diabetes pregnancy. *Diabetes Care, 30*, 161–168.

Harvard Medical School (2005). Perimenopause: Rocky road to menopause: Symptoms we call "menopausal" often precede menopause by years. *Harvard Women's Health Watch, 12* (12), 1–4.

Heffner, L., & Schust, D. (2006). *Reproductive systems at a glance*, 2nd ed. Ames, IA: Blackwell Publishing Professional.

Henshaw, S. K. (1998). Unintended pregnancy in the United States. *Family Planning Perspectives, 30*, 24–29.

Hersey, J., Anliker, J., Miller, Ch., Mullis, R. M., Daugherty, S., Das, S., Bray, C. R., Dennee, P., Sigman-Grant, M., & Thomas, H. O. (2001). Food shopping practices are associated with dietary quality in low-income households. *Journal of Nutrition Education, 33*, s16–s26.

Hogan, M., Foreman, K., Naghavi, M., Ahn, S., Wang, M., Makela, S., Lopez, A., Lozano, R., & Murray, C. (2010). Maternal mortality for 181 countries, 1980–2008: A systematic analysis of progress towards millennium development goal 5. *The Lancet, 375*(9726), 1609–1623.

Honey, E., & Templeton, A. (2002). Prevention of pelvic inflammatory disease by the control of *C. trachomatis* infection. *International Journal of Gynecology & Obstetrics, 78*(3), 257–261.

Institute of Medicine (1990). *Nutrition during pregnancy: Part I: Nutritional status and weight gain*. Washington, D.C.: National Academies Press.

Jernstrom, H., Lubinski, J., Lynch, H., et al. (2004). Breast-feeding and the risk of breast cancer in BRCA1 and BRCA2 mutation carriers. *Journal of the National Cancer Institute, 96,* 1094–1098.

Jones, R., & Henshaw, S. (2002). Mifepristone for early medical abortion: Experiences in France, Great Britain, and Sweden. *Perspectives on Sexual & Reproductive Health, 34*(3), 154–161.

Jones, R., & Kooistra, K. (2011). Abortion incidence and access to services in the United States 2008. *Perspectives on Sexual & Reproductive Health, 43*(1), 41–50.

Jones, R., & Lopez, K. (2006). *Human Reproductive Biology,* 3rd ed. Burlington, MA: Elsevier.

Jones, R., Zolna, M., Stanley K., Henshaw, S., & Finer, L. (2008). Abortion in the United States: Incidence and access to services 2005. *Perspectives on Sexual & Reproductive Health, 40*(1), 6–16.

Kim, C., Sinco, B., & Kieffer, E. (2007). Racial and ethnic variation in access to health care, provision of health care services, and ratings of health among women with histories of gestational diabetes mellitus. *Diabetes Care, 30,* 1459–1465.

Kim, S., Dietz, P., England, L., Morrow, B., & Callaghan, W. (2007). Trends in pre-pregnancy obesity in nine states, 1993–2003. *Obesity, 15,* 986–993.

Kogan, M., Alexander, G., Kotelchuck, M., Macdorman, M., Buckens, P., Martin, J., & Papiernik, E. (2000). Trends in twin birth outcomes and prenatal care utilization in the United States, 1981-1997. *The Journal of American Medical Association, 284*(3), 335-341.

Kung H., Hoyert D., Xu J., & Murphy S. (2008). Deaths: Final data for 2005. *National Vital Statistics Reports, 56*(10). Hyattsville, MD: National Center for Health Statistics.

Martin, J., Hamilton, B., Sutton, P., Ventura, S., Menacker, F., Kirmeyer, S., Mathews, T. (2009). Births: Final data for 2006. *National Vital Statistics Reports, 57*(7). Hyattsville, MD: National Center for Health Statistics.

MacDorman, M., & Mathews, T. (2008). Recent trends in infant mortality in the United States. *NCHS Data Brief, 9.* Hyattsville, MD: National Center for Health Statistics.

Mathews, T., & MacDorman, M. (2010). Infant mortality statistics from the 2006 period linked birth/infant death data set. *National Vital Statistics Reports, 58*(17). Hyattsville, MD: National Center for Health Statistics.

McClure, E., Nalubamba-Phiri, M., & Goldenberg, R. (2006). Stillbirth in developing countries. *International Journal of Gynecology & Obstetrics, 94(2),* 82–90.

McCormick, M., Sanghvi, H., Kinzie, B., & McIntosh, N. (2002). Averting maternal death and disability: Preventing postpartum hemorrhage in low-resource settings. *International Journal of Gynecology & Obstetrics, 77,* 267–275.

McDowell, M., Wang, C., & Kennedy-Stephenson, J. (2008). Breastfeeding in the United States: Findings from the National Health and Nutrition Examination Survey, 1999-2006. *NCHS Data Brief, 5.* Hyattsville, MD: National Center for Health Statistics.

Menacker, F., & Hamilton, B. (2010). Recent trends in cesarean delivery in the United States. *NCHS Data Brief, 35.* Hyattsville, MD: National Center for Health Statistics.

Morland, K., Wing, S., & Diez, R. A. (2002). The contextual effect of the local food environment on residents' diets: The Atherosclerosis Risk in Communities study. *American Journal of Public Health, 92,* 1761–1767.

Mosher, W., & Jones, J. (2010). Use of contraception in the United States: 1982–2008. *Vital Health Statistics, 23*(29). Hyattsville, MD: National Center for Health Statistics.

Mosley, B., Cleves, M., Siega-Riz, A., Shaw, G., Canfield, M., Waller, D., Werler, M., Hobbs, C. et al. (2009). Neural tube defects and maternal folate intake among pregnancies conceived after folic acid fortification in the United States. *American Journal of Epidemiology, 169*(1), 9–17.

Murphy, H., Rayman, G., Lewis, K., Kelly, S., Johal, B., Duffield, K., Fowler, D., Campbell, P., & Temple, R. (2008). Effectiveness of continuous glucose monitoring in pregnant women with diabetes: Randomized clinical trial. *British Medical Journal, 337,* 1680–1687.

Myles, T., Gooch, J., & Santolaya, J. (2002). Obesity as an independent risk factor for infectious morbidity in patients who undergo cesarean delivery. *Obstetrics & Gynecology, 100,* 959–964.

National Center for Health Statistics. (2005). *Births: Final data for 2003.* Vital statistics of the United States. Available at: http://www.cdc.gov/nchs/data/nvsr/nvsr54/nvsr54_02.pdf. Accessed December 1, 2010.

Ogden, C. L., Carroll, M. D., Curtin, L. R., McDowell, M. A., Tabak, C. J., Flegal, K. M. (2006). Prevalence of overweight and obesity in the United States, 1999-2004. *JAMA 295,* 1549–1555.

Olson, C., Strawderman, M., Hinton, P., & Pearson, T. (2003). Gestational weight gain and postpartum behaviors associated with weight change from early pregnancy to 1 y postpartum. *International Journal of Obesity, 27,* 117–127.

O'Toole, M. L., Sawicki, M. A., & Artal, R. (2003). Structured Diet and Physical Activity Prevent Postpartum Weight Retention. *Journal of Women's Health, 2,* 991–998.

Pazol, K., Gamble, S., Parker, W., Cook, D., Zane, S., & Hamdan, S. (2009). Abortion surveillance—United States 2006. *Morbidity & Mortality Weekly Report, 58*(SS08), 1–35.

Power, M., Cogswell, M., & Schulkin, J. (2006). Obesity prevention and treatment practices of U.S. obstetrician-gynecologists. *Obstetrics & Gynecology, 108,* 961–968.

Rasmussen, K. M., & Yaktine, A. L. (2009). *Weight gain during pregnancy: Reexamining the guidelines.* Washington, D.C.: National Academies Press.

Robinson, H., O'Connell, C., Joseph, K., & McLeod, N. (2005). Maternal outcomes in pregnancies complicated by obesity. *Obstetrics & Gynecology, 106,* 1357–1364.

Roelands, J., Jamison, M., Lyerly, A., & James, A. (2009). Consequences of smoking during pregnancy on maternal health. *Journal of Women's Health, 18*(6), 867–872.

Rosenn, B. (2008). Obesity and diabetes: A recipe for obstetric complications. *Journal of Maternal-Fetal and Neonatal Medicine, 21,* 159-164.

Siega-Riz, A. M., & Laraia, B. (2006). The Implications of maternal overweight and obesity on the course of pregnancy and birth outcomes. *Maternal & Child Health Journal, 10,* 153–156.

Siega-Riz, A. M., Rodnar, L. M. & Savitz, D. A. (2002). What are pregnant women eating? Nutrient and food group differences by race. *American Journal of Obstetrics & Gynecology, 186,* 480–486.

Spandorfer, S., Avrech, O., Colombero, L., Palermo, G., & Rosenwaks, Z. (1998). Effect of parental age on fertilization and pregnancy characteristics in couples treated by intracytoplasmic sperm injection. *Human Reproduction, 13,* 334–338.

Stotland, N., Haas, J., Brawarsky, P., Jackson, R., Fuentes-Afflick, E., & Escobar, G. (2005). Body mass index, provider advice and target gestational weight gain. *Obstetrics & Gynecology, 105,* 633–638.

The Guttmacher Institute. (2011). *In brief: Facts on induced abortion in the United States.* New York, NY: The Guttmacher Institute.

The World Bank. (2007). *Maternal mortality in 2005: Estimates developed by WHO, UNICEF, UNFPA, and the World Bank.* Geneva, CH: The World Bank.

Ventura, S., Abma, J., Mosher, W., & Henshaw, S. (2009). Estimated pregnancy rates for the United States, 1990–2005: An update. *National Vital Statistics Reports, 58*(4). Hyattsville, MD: National Center for Health Statistics.

Wilcox, A., Baird, D., & Weinberg, C. (1999). Time of implantation of the conceptus and loss of pregnancy. *New England Journal of Medicine, 340,* 1796–1799.

Yogev, Y., & Visser, G. (2009). Obesity, gestational diabetes and pregnancy outcome. *Seminars in Fetal & Neonatal Medicine, 14,* 77–84.

Zhang, C., Solomon, C., Manson, J., & Hu, F. (2006). A prospective study of pregravid physical activity and sedentary behaviors in relation to the risk of gestational diabetes mellitus. *Archives of Internal Medicine, 166,* 543–548.

Zhu, J., Madsen, K., Vestergaard, M., Olesen, A., Basso, O., & Olsen, J. (2005). Paternal age and congenital malformations. *Human Reproduction 20*(11), 3173–3177.

CHAPTER

10

Reproductive Tract Infections

OBJECTIVES: STUDENTS WILL BE ABLE TO

1. Recognize how RTIs can negatively impact one's reproductive health.
2. Distinguish between bacterial and viral sexually transmitted infections.
3. List three ways to decrease the risk of exposure of sexually transmitted infections.
4. Apply critical thinking skill Level 5, Synthesis.

FROM VD TO RTIs: A HISTORICAL PERSPECTIVE

The adjective word *venereal* (from the Latin word *venereus,* meaning desire or love) is defined as "transmitted by sexual intercourse" in the American Heritage Dictionary. For hundreds of years, syphilis (which was known as the "pox") and gonorrhea (which was known as the "clap") were two of the most common venereal diseases (VD) known to exist (McGough, 2008; Rosebury, 1971). It wasn't until the 1940s that syphilis and gonorrhea were reined in by the discovery of penicillin. During the 1960s, when 20 other diseases were recognized as being transmitted by sexual contact, public health officials in the United States introduced a new term, *sexually transmitted diseases* (STDs), to replace venereal disease in an effort to improve the clarity of their warnings to the public.

The American Heritage Stedman's Medical Dictionary defines the word *disease* as "a pathological condition of a body part, an organ, or a system resulting from various causes, such as infection, genetic defect, or environmental stress, and characterized by an identifiable group of signs or symptoms." Because numerous STDs were found to be asymptomatic to at least 50 percent of those infected, a new term was created in the 1990s to help clarify a long-standing misconception that people who have an STD are aware of their status because they would have the symptoms for it. With over 30 infections identified as primarily being acquired through (unprotected) sexual activity, this new term, *sexually transmitted infections* (STIs), was also introduced to try to reduce the stigma attached with being diagnosed with an STD (Moore & Moore, 2005).

A new term surfaced in the mid-1990s in order to highlight the pathogens' role in minimizing sexual and reproductive health, as well as to move away from blaming sexual behavior and individuals. *Reproductive tract infections (RTIs)* was re-introduced by the editors of the eighteenth edition of *Contraceptive Technology* (Cates, 2004). The term *RTIs* is used alongside *STIs* in international organizations such as the World Health Organization (WHO), Engender Health, and the Population Council, to name a few. According to WHO (2005), RTIs refer to three different types of infections that affect the reproductive tract. Table 10.1 highlights the differences between these infections.

REPRODUCTIVE TRACT INFECTIONS

Not all sexually transmitted infections are reproductive tract infections, and not all reproductive tract infections are sexually transmitted. Even so, the three types of RTIs mentioned in Table 10.1 overlap and should be considered together. For example, some STIs, such as gonorrhea or chlamydia, can be spread to the upper reproductive tract if left untreated and may lead to pelvic inflammatory disease (PID), an iatrogenic infection. In addition, some endogenous infections, such as bacterial vaginosis, can also lead to PID if not properly treated. According to Hillier and her colleagues (2008), bacterial vaginosis (BV), gonorrhea, or chlamydia can ascend into the reproductive tract during a procedure, such as an IUD insertion, and if left untreated, may cause PID.

According to Cates (2004), regardless of mode of transmission, RTIs have four serious health consequences: (1) a blockage of one or both of the fallopian tubes leading to infertility and ectopic pregnancy; (2) pregnancy loss and neonatal morbidity caused by transmission of the infection to the fetus during pregnancy and birth; (3) geni-

TABLE 10.1: Types of Reproductive Tract Infections

RTI	CONSEQUENCES
Endogenous infections	Probably the most common RTIs worldwide, they occur from an overgrowth of organisms normally present in the vagina. These infections are not usually sexually transmitted and include bacterial vaginosis and candidiasis. They can be easily treated and cured.
Iatrogenic infections	These infections occur when a bacterium or other microorganism is introduced into the upper reproductive tract by a medical procedure such as endometrial biopsy, induced abortion, IUD insertion, or birth. This can happen because the infection already present in the lower reproductive tract is pushed or allowed entry through the cervix into the upper reproductive tract.
Sexually transmitted infections (STIs)	Sexually transmitted infections (STIs) are caused by viruses, bacteria, or parasitic microorganisms that are transmitted through (unprotected) sexual activity with an infected partner. Some STIs can be easily treated, such as gonorrhea and chlamydia. Other STIs, such as the human immunodeficiency virus (HIV) and herpes simplex virus-2 (known as genital herpes), are not curable.

tal cancers, such as cervical and penile cancer; and (4) easier transmission of HIV. Any STI that produces genital lesions (such as genital herpes and syphilis) or induces an inflammatory reaction places the individual at risk of acquiring HIV. Moreover, numerous infections, such as BV, chlamydia, genital herpes, and syphilis, have been found to alter vaginal and cervical defenses that can lead to women being more susceptible to HIV (Hillier, Marrazzo & Holmes, 2008).

Given the transmission dynamics of coitus, women are more likely than men to acquire an RTI from any single sexual encounter (Cates, 2004). According to Buve and her colleagues (2008), when compared to men, women are more likely to suffer from severe long-term consequences due to RTIs, such as PID, infertility, ectopic pregnancy and cervical cancer.

RTIs DURING PREGNANCY

According to Goldenberg and his colleagues (1997), some RTIs, such as genital herpes and BV, are frequently diagnosed in pregnant women in the United States. Table 10.2 shows the estimated number of women in the United States who are diagnosed during their pregnancy with specific RTIs each year (CDC, 2011).

For some women, a positive diagnosis of an RTI during the pregnancy does not necessarily mean that they were infected during the pregnancy. Many women do not routinely seek RTI screening during their lifetime. Yet many women agree to be screened during their pregnancy, either to ensure a healthy pregnancy or because it is a required clinical assessment at the prenatal clinic. Moreover, because a woman's immune system is compromised during pregnancy, it is also possible that such decreased immunity provides an opportunity for symptoms to occur (Watts, 2008). For example, as shown in Table 10.2, there are a high number of pregnant women diagnosed with genital herpes during pregnancy. Yet, it is not believed that all these women were infected with HSV-2 during pregnancy.

TABLE 10.2: U.S. Females Diagnosed with RTIs during Pregnancy

RTI	ESTIMATED NUMBER OF PREGNANT WOMEN PER YEAR
Bacterial vaginosis	1,080,000
Genital herpes	880,000
Chlamydia	100,000
Trichomoniasis	124,000
Gonorrhea	13,200
HIV	6,400
Syphilis	<1,000

PELVIC INFLAMMATORY DISEASE (PID)

PID is an umbrella term for a variety of infections of the upper reproductive organs, including the ovaries, the fallopian tubes (salpingitis), the endometrial lining of the uterus (endometritis), the uterine wall, as well as the ligaments that support the uterus, and even the lining of the abdomen (Paavonen, Westrom, & Eschenbach, 2008). Because severe cellular damage of the fallopian tubes can result from PID, such a condition has also been associated with irregular bleeding, chronic pelvic pain, infertility and ectopic pregnancy (Haggerty, Schulz, & Ness, 2003).

© 2011 by Kalim. Used under license of Shutterstock, Inc.

Because women can be infected over and over again with chlamydia, gonorrhea, and BV, PID can occur multiple times as well. These RTIs can be cured, but that doesn't mean a person is immune from future exposure. Ectopic pregnancy is the leading cause of first-trimester, pregnancy-related deaths in American women (Paavonen, Westrom, & Eschenbach, 2008). Moreover, with every episode of PID that a woman is diagnosed with during her lifetime, she increases her risk of becoming infertile. PID is curable, but any damage done to the reproductive organs or surrounding tissues cannot be reversed (Wiesenfeld & Cates, 2008).

Every year, it is estimated that more than 1 million women experience an episode of acute PID in the United States (CDC, 2002). More than 100,000 women become infertile each year as a result of PID, and a large proportion of the ectopic pregnancies occurring every year are due to the consequences of PID. Annually, more than 150 American women die from PID or its complications (Paavonen, Westrom, & Eschenbach, 2008).

SEXUALLY TRANSMITTED INFECTIONS

The most recent national estimates, now over a decade old, estimate the total number of people living in the United States with a viral STI to be over 65 million (American Social Health Association, 1998). Every year, there are at least 19 million new cases of STIs in the United States (Weinstock, Berman & Cates, 2004). Although young adults (15–24 year-olds) represent only one-quarter of the sexually active population, they account for nearly half of all new STIs each year (Weinstock, Berman & Cates, 2004).

One in four women will be infected with an STI during her lifetime, with most of these infections occurring during young adulthood (Garnett, 2008). Estimates of the incidence (new cases) and prevalence (total existing cases) of most STIs are difficult to make, though, because so many people do not exhibit any symptoms and thus do not seek screening or treatment.

BACTERIAL INFECTIONS

Bacterial infections that are sexually transmitted are curable with antibiotics, thereby reducing any negative health consequences for an individual, as well as reducing the ability for that person to infect others. That doesn't mean, though, that the person cannot be reinfected again in the future. Moreover, possible damage caused to any reproductive organs by a bacterial STI cannot be reversed even if one is cured of that infection. Prompt medical attention is needed to decrease the chances of the bacteria ascending past the vagina of females, or urethra of females and males.

Unfortunately, 50 percent to 80 percent of individuals infected with an STI will not show symptoms and will probably not seek testing and treatment. Transmitting these STIs is possible, with or without symptoms. It is better to get tested and find out you are not infected, than to realize you have an STI after damage has occurred to your reproductive organs which could complicate your ability to procreate in the future. The bacterial infections that will be discussed below are chlamydia, gonorrhea and syphilis.

CHLAMYDIA

Chlamydia is the most reported bacterial STI in the United States, with over 1 million cases documented in 2007 (CDC, 2008d). This STI is believed to be grossly underreported because 75 percent of women and 50 percent of men infected with chlamydia do not exhibit any symptoms of the infection and thus will not seek treatment (Stamm, 2008).

Symptoms include abdominal pain and a burning sensation when urinating in women and men, urethral discharge in men, vaginal discharge in women and rectal pain, and discharge and bleeding in women and men participating in receptive anal intercourse (Stamm, 2008). These symptoms can present themselves anywhere from one to three weeks after exposure. Symptoms can disappear without treatment, which can lead to a false sense of security that your body took care of the infection or nothing was really wrong with you to begin with.

In both sexes, the urethra, mouth, throat, eyes and anus can be infected. In women, chlamydia can infect the cervix, uterus, and fallopian tubes. Ten to 40 percent of untreated chlamydia cases will lead to PID, and as many as 20 percent of women with PID will become infertile (CDC, 2009). Interestingly, chlamydial infection of the cervix can spread to the rectum. In males, chlamydia can infect the epididymis and prostate gland, which can cause discomfort, pain, and rarely sterility.

Chlamydia can be transmitted during coitus, anal intercourse, or oral sex, as well as passed on to the fetus by an infected mother during vaginal birth. This bacterium can be inhaled by the baby during birth and cause the baby to be born with a form of pneumonia that requires antibiotics at birth to prevent further health complications (Kohlhoff & Hammerschlag, 2008). It is recommended for sexually active women 25 years and younger to be screened at least annually for chlamydia and for all pregnant women to ask to be tested for chlamydia early in their prenatal care (Stamm, 2008). Annual screening is not recommended for males even though it is in every sexually active man's best interest to be tested!

GONORRHEA

Over 350,000 cases of gonorrhea were reported in the United States in 2007 (CDC, 2008d). It is believed that the actual number of cases is around 700,000. Similar to chlamydia, the majority of women (80 percent) and half of all men infected with gonorrhea do not exhibit any symptoms.

Symptoms can take as long as 30 days to appear. For men, symptoms include a burning sensation when urinating, or a white, yellow, or green discharge from the penis. Gonorrhea can cause epididymitis, a painful condition of the ducts attached to the testicles that may lead to infertility if left untreated (Geisler & Krieger, 2008). Symptoms in women include a painful or burning sensation when urinating, increased vaginal discharge, or vaginal bleeding between periods. Symptoms of rectal infection in both women and men may include discharge, anal itching, soreness, bleeding, or painful bowel movements.

This bacterium has been found to grow and multiply easily in warm, moist areas. In the female reproductive tract, these areas include the cervix, uterus, and fallopian tubes. Gonorrhea can also grow in the mouth, throat, eyes, urethra, and anus in women and men. Interestingly, ejaculation does not have to occur to transmit or become infected with gonorrhea. This microorganism can also be spread from mother to baby during vaginal birth. This exposure can cause blindness, joint infection, or a life-threatening blood infection in the baby (Kohlhoff & Hammerschlag, 2008).

SYPHILIS

Over 36,000 cases of syphilis were reported in the United States in 2006 (CDC, 2008d). Incidence was highest in women 20 to 24 years of age and in men 35 to 39 years of age. The majority of cases occurred between men who have sex with men. Reported cases of congenital syphilis in newborns increased to 349 cases in 2006 from 339 cases in 2005. Because serious complications (even death) can occur to babies infected with syphilis, this is the only STI that has a federal mandate for testing during prenatal care of all women in the United States (Hansfield, 2008). Moreover, a positive diagnosis of syphilis is required to be reported to state health departments and the Centers of Disease Control and Prevention (CDC).

Transmission of the organism occurs during coitus, anal intercourse, or oral sex. Syphilis is passed from person to person through direct contact with a syphilis sore. Sores occur mainly on the vulva, penis, scrotum, vagina, anus, or in the rectum. Sores also can occur on the lips and in the mouth.

Syphilis has four stages, which vary in length, symptoms, and severity of health complications. A person can only be cured during the first two stages of syphilis. A person is not curable during the third and fourth stage. In all four stages a person can infect another individual through blood or to the fetus through the placenta during pregnancy, but a person can transmit the organism sexually only during the first two stages (Sparling et al., 2008).

The primary stage is the first stage of this STI. During this stage, a sore (called a chancre) appears in the area where the organism entered the body (Sparling et al., 2008). Because this sore is painless, an individual might not realize that she or he is infected with syphilis. Moreover, if a person is unaware of the symptoms or signs associated with syphilis, she or he may not believe she or he is infected with an STI. The chancre can appear anywhere from 10 to 90 days after exposure. The chancre associated with primary syphilis lasts 3 to 6 weeks, and it heals without treatment. However, the infection progresses to the secondary stage if treatment is not provided (Sparling et al., 2008).

During the secondary stage, a non-itchy skin rash can occur throughout the body, but it is very prominent in palms of the hands and soles of the feet (Sparling et al., 2008). This skin rash can appear anywhere from 2 to 10 weeks after the disappearance of the chancre. The lesions created by the skin rash contain the syphilis bacterium, and thus, others can be infected by touch. The signs and symptoms of secondary syphilis will resolve without treatment, and the infection will progress to the latent and possibly the tertiary (or last) stage (Sparling et al., 2008).

During the latent (or third) stage of syphilis, there are no observable signs or symptoms of infection (Sparling et al., 2008). Unfortunately, during this stage the bacterium invades the internal organs, including the brain, nerves, eyes, heart, blood vessels, liver, bones, and joints. Around 15 percent of people who have not been treated for syphilis will develop the late stages of syphilis (Sparling et al., 2008). This can occur 10 to 20 years after infection was first acquired.

The fourth and last stage of syphilis is called the tertiary stage. Given the irreversible damage that occurs to the internal organs during the latent stage, many in this stage can experience blindness, insanity, paralysis, and death (Douglas, 2009).

VIRAL INFECTIONS

Viral infections that are sexually transmitted are *not* curable. That means we do not have medication that can cure an individual, but we do have medication that can alleviate any complications that can arise from these STIs, and for some, these medications can also reduce the risk of transmission to a sexual partner (Winer & Koutsky, 2008). Transmitting these STIs is possible, with or without symptoms. Fluid transmission, such as seminal and vaginal fluid, is not always necessary to acquire these infections (Corey & Wald, 2008; Winer & Koutsky, 2008). The viral STIs that will be discussed here are genital herpes (herpes simplex virus-2), human papillomavirus (HPV), and human immunodeficiency virus (HIV). Oral herpes (herpes simplex virus-1) will also be discussed, even though it is not considered an STI. As stated earlier, skin-to-skin contact can transmit certain STIs to one another. Of the STIs discussed here, only HIV cannot be transmitted through skin-to-skin contact.

HERPES SIMPLEX VIRUS-1 (ORAL HERPES)

Around 80 percent of the U.S. population is believed to be infected with oral herpes. Surprised? Ever heard of "cold sores" or "fever blisters"? Well, that's oral herpes. Oral herpes belongs to the herpes family of more than 100 viruses, which includes not only oral and genital herpes (discussed below), but also herpes varicella zoster, the virus that causes chicken pox and shingles, and Epstein–Barr, the virus that causes mononucleosis, also known as "mono" or the "kissing disease" (Pertel & Spear, 2008).

The majority of us did not acquire oral herpes by sexual transmission, and most of us weren't even sexually active when the first infamous, painful sore appeared by our lips! Many of us unknowingly became infected by a kiss by a well-meaning relative during our childhood or adolescence. This virus takes up residence in the trigeminal ganglion, a collection of nerve cells near the ear (Pertel & Spear, 2008).

Many outbreaks occur when a person has a cold or a fever, which usually means your immune system is weakened due to an illness and this virus takes advantage to try and transmit to other "hosts". Before an outbreak, many individuals experience a tingling, burning, or itching sensation around the lips or inside the mouth (this is considered viral shedding). Viral shedding is a release of infectious viral particles from the affected site. Not everyone who experiences viral shedding has symptoms though, yet she or he can still transmit the virus to others (Pertel & Spear, 2008), and a day or two later, a sore appears at the site. People have also been known to experience an outbreak after

Herpesvirus varicella-zoster

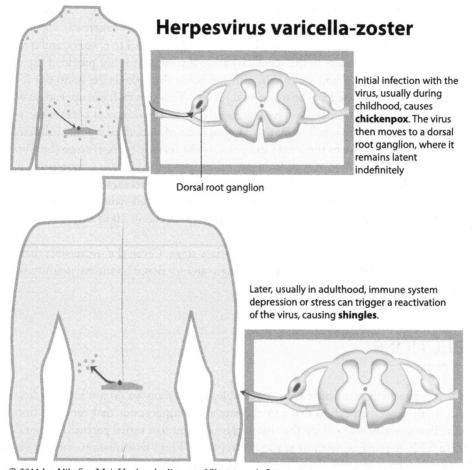

Initial infection with the virus, usually during childhood, causes **chickenpox**. The virus then moves to a dorsal root ganglion, where it remains latent indefinitely

Dorsal root ganglion

Later, usually in adulthood, immune system depression or stress can trigger a reactivation of the virus, causing **shingles**.

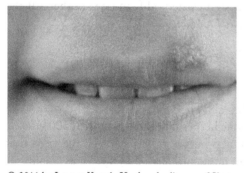

they've eaten spicy foods, gotten sunburned on their face, or when they are stressed out. Women can also experience an outbreak during a pregnancy and along with hormonal changes during the menstrual cycle. It is unknown how those occurrences cause an outbreak.

Very effective, over-the-counter medication exists for oral herpes that can shorten the duration of an outbreak and reduce viral shedding. There are some prescription drugs that can eliminate outbreaks altogether. Even though most "cold sores" are believed to come from herpes simplex virus-1, it is possible for a person to be infected with herpes simplex virus-2 (the virus that causes genital herpes) instead (Pertel & Spear, 2008). Even when an infected person is asymptomatic, she or he can pass on oral herpes through viral shedding. For those prone to regular outbreaks, oral herpes can be a downright annoying experience and can cause individuals to be self-conscious. Oral herpes can be transmitted to the genitals through oral sex, and this infection is much more life-altering, painful, and stressful with which to cope.

HERPES SIMPLEX VIRUS-2 (GENITAL HERPES)

Around 16 percent of people in the United States are infected with genital herpes (CDC, 2008d). Genital herpes is more common in women (1 in 6) than in men (1 in 9). It is believed that 25 percent of people infected with genital

Herpesvirus (type 1) Infection

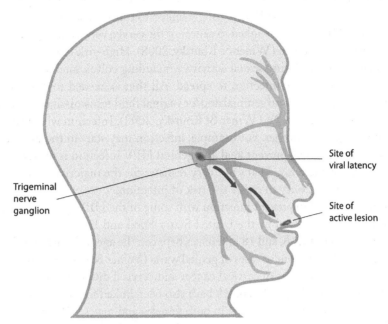

© 2011 by Alila Sao Mai. Used under license of Shutterstock, Inc.

herpes do not know they have it because they have never had an outbreak (Corey & Wald, 2008). Within two weeks of exposure, an individual's first outbreak may occur. In genital herpes, the virus resides in the sacral ganglion at the base of the spine (Pertel & Spear, 2008). There, the virus stays dormant until a weakened immune system allows it to flare up again in the skin, usually in the genital area.

Even though there is no cure for genital herpes, three medications (available by prescription only) currently on the market, Acyclovir®, Famciclovir®, and Valaciclovir®, are equally effective at preventing or treating outbreaks. These medications work by inhibiting an enzyme needed for the virus to replicate (Corey & Wald, 2008). Because these drugs travel through the bloodstream, they cannot eradicate the infection at its source. Thus, the only time the medications can attack the virus is when it is headed back toward the skin, which is infused by blood vessels, to cause another outbreak (Corey & Wald, 2008). Because no one really knows when another outbreak will occur, an individual has to take the medication every single day, with or without symptoms.

A pregnant woman can expose the fetus to the virus, especially if the woman is infected during the third trimester (Bradford, Whitley & Stagno, 2008). Exposure can occur in utero or as the baby passes through the vaginal canal during birth. The health complications to the baby can be quite severe and can lead to death (Bradford, Whitley & Stagno, 2008).

HUMAN PAPILLOMAVIRUS (HPV)

HPV infects about 6 million people in the United States each year. The majority of these cases resolve on their own and no medical intervention is needed. Even so, the most important risk factor for cervical cancer is an HPV infection. HPV is a group of more than 100 related viruses that only infect cells on the surface of the skin, genitals, anus, mouth and throat, but not the blood or most internal organs such as the heart or lungs (Winer & Koutsky, 2008). These viruses are called papilloma viruses because some of them cause a type of growth called a papilloma, which are more commonly known as warts.

Different types of HPV cause warts on different parts of the body. Some cause common warts on the hands and feet; others tend to cause warts on the lips or tongue. Still other types of HPV may cause warts on or around the female and male external genitals and in the anal area (Winer & Koutsky, 2008). These warts may barely be visible or they may be several inches across. These are known as genital warts or condyloma acuminatum. HPV 6 and HPV 11 are the two types of HPV that cause most cases of genital warts. They are called "low-risk" types of HPV because they are seldom linked to cancer. Certain types of HPV are strongly linked to cancers and are considered "high-risk" types. As discussed in Chapters 6 and 7, HPV has been linked to cancer of the cervix, vulva, and vagina, as well the penis and anal and throat cancer in both women and men (Winer & Koutsky, 2008). High-risk types include 16, 18, 31, 33, and 45.

Although HPV can be spread during sexual activity—including coitus, anal intercourse, and oral sex—none of these behaviors have to occur for the infection to spread. All that is needed to pass HPV from one person to another is skin-to-skin contact (meaning no seminal and/or vaginal fluid transmission is needed to become infected) with an area of the body infected with HPV (Winer & Koutsky, 2008). Infection with HPV seems to be able to be spread from one part of the body to another. For example, infection may start in the vagina and then spread to the cervix. The only sure way to completely prevent anal and genital HPV infection is to never allow another person to have contact with those areas of the body. That's not very realistic for the majority of the U.S. population, though. Thus, consistent condom use is necessary to *reduce* the risk of infection.

Vaccines have been developed to prevent infection with some of the HPV types associated with cervical cancer and genital warts. Gardasil® was approved by the United States Food and Drug Administration (FDA) in 2006 to produce immunity to HPV types 6, 11, 16, and 18 in females between the ages of 9 and 26 (CDC, 2007). The first two types are known to cause around 90 percent of cases of genital warts (Winer & Koutsky, 2008). The latter two types are known to cause around 70 percent of cases of cervical cancer and cervical dysplasia (precancerous changes of cervical cells, which can linger for years). HPV types 16 and 18 have also been linked to precancerous lesions and cancer of the vulva and vagina in females and the anus and throat in both females and males (Winer & Koutsky, 2008). Cervarix® was approved by the FDA in 2009 to produce immunity to HPV types 16 and 18 only. Cervarix® is approved for use in females between the ages of 10 to 25 years. Vaccinated women who are exposed to these viruses should not develop infections. At this time, immunity can only be guaranteed for five years with either of these vaccines.

In 2009, Gardasil® was approved by the FDA to produce immunity to HPV types 6 and 11 in males between the ages of 9 and 26. In late 2010, the FDA approved the use of Gardasil® to prevent anal cancer and precancerous lesions. Even though this approval is meant to decrease anal cancer in men who have sex with men, there's no reason not to believe that Gardasil® can also prevent anal cancer in women who participate in this sexual behavior with men. These vaccinations are believed to be most effective if an individual is not infected with any of the HPV types the vaccine protects a person from (even though some immunity is possible with the types that a person does not have). Both Cervarix® and Gardasil® requires a series of three injections over a six-month period (first dose, then two months later, then in the sixth month after the first dose).

There are other HPV types that can cause precancerous lesions, cancer, or genital warts that you are not protected against by being vaccinated (Winer & Koutsky, 2008). Thus, condoms must be used consistently with every type of sexual act to prevent fluid transmission and skin-to-skin contact to *reduce* risk. If used properly, male condoms can protect the penis and wherever the penis ends up in. This can be the vagina, the cervix, the anus, the rectum, the mouth, and the throat. If used properly, female condoms can protect the vagina, the cervix and the penis. The vulva of a female and the scrotum of a male are not protected with female or male condoms. These areas can be infected with STIs that can be passed on through skin-to-skin contact, like HPV.

HUMAN IMMUNODEFICIENCY VIRUS (HIV)

In the early 1980s, a new disease infecting primarily men who had sex with men raised red flags throughout the medical community in the United States and soon after, around the world. Interestingly, the first known HIV infection was identified in a man from the Democratic Republic of Congo in 1959 (Jones & Lopez, 2006). It became apparent very quickly that this disease afflicted not just men who had sex with men, but men who had sex with women, intravenous drug users, and newborns (infected by their mothers in utero or at birth). This virus, known as HIV, is the virus known to cause acquired immunodeficiency disease (AIDS). HIV can be transmitted through blood, seminal and vaginal fluids, and breast milk of an HIV+ person (American Social Health Association, 2009). Seminal fluid has the highest concentration of HIV (Jones & Lopez, 2006).

More than 1.6 million Americans have been infected with HIV since initial documentation began for this infection. More than 540,000 have already died since the first reported case in 1981. Around 56,000 new HIV infections occur each year, a number that has remained stable since 2000 (CDC, 2008a). Eighty percent of women diagnosed with HIV/AIDS in 2006 contracted the virus through heterosexual contact (CDC, 2008b). An HIV+ man is 18 times more likely to infect a woman through sexual activity than the other way around (Jones & Lopez, 2006). In 2006, as many as one in five individuals with HIV may have been unaware of their HIV+ status, down from one in four in 2003 (CDC, 2008c). HIV infection disproportionately affects the African-American community, especially African-American women.

Numerous drugs have been developed to delay the onset of AIDS. There are currently four classes of drugs used to prevent replication of the virus. A combination of these drugs has been found to be most effective in slowing the progression of the disease and prolonging life (Jones & Lopez, 2006). A vaccine to prevent HIV or even to cure individuals already infected has been under study for decades, yet such a development continues to elude the research community. One reason for this is that the virus is known to mutate, making development of a vaccine difficult. There are now 15 known mutations that exist for HIV (Jones & Lopez, 2006). Although AIDS doesn't kill the person, bacterial and viral infections take advantage of the person's compromised immune system and such opportunitistic infections can lead to a person's death.

PREVENTION OF RTIs

What happens if you are diagnosed with chlamydia? You have been in a monogamous relationship for three months, yet both of you had sexual partners in the past. Could your recent partner have cheated on you? Did you? Or could either of you have brought this infection into the relationship? All three scenarios are possible. Screening and treatment of your partner is crucial not only to improving your own health, but to break the cycle of reinfection that is commonly seen among patients with bacterial infections such as gonorrhea and chlamydia. Because it is often complicated to get someone's partner (or partners) to get tested and treated, many professionals in the STI field recommend that the infected partner's health care clinician provide the patient a supply of or prescription for antibiotics to the partner that was not tested.

One of three most effective ways to avoid acquiring an STI is to abstain from all sexual activity. That means no penis in a vagina, no penis in a rectum, no penis in a mouth, and no vulva on the tongue or lips! Because only skin-to-skin contact is needed to transmit some STIs, the genitals of another person should not be touching yours.

What if abstinence is not an option because you want to be sexually active? Well, another way to avoid acquiring an STI is to be in a long-term, mutually monogamous relationship with a partner who does not have an STI. If that is not possible at this time, then a third way to reduce your risk of coming into contact with an STI is to use condoms. For condoms to be effective, they need to be used consistently and correctly with each and every episode of sexual activity.

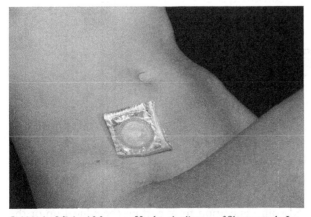

© 2011 by Michael Macsuga. Used under license of Shutterstock, Inc.

© 2011 by lenetstan. Used under license of Shutterstock, Inc.

PSYCHOSOCIAL RESPONSES TO STIs

People's reactions vary considerably when they find out they have an STI. Some people are very nonchalant about the whole event, while others are completely horrified. How do you think you'd respond to such a diagnosis? Would it matter if you had multiple sexual partners; or were in a monogamous long-term relationship; or if it happened because of a "one-night stand"? Would you respond differently if you were 15, 21, 35, or 65 years old? Ross (1986) theorized four separate meanings that individuals can place on their STI diagnosis and why it occurred:

1. STIs are a deserved outcome of indiscriminate sexual behavior and punishment for sexual sins.
2. STIs are a consequence of individual inadequacy that leads to sexually indiscriminate behavior.
3. STIs are a consequence of a breakdown in traditional social values and rapid social change.
4. STIs are solely the result of an individual coming into intimate contact with a virulent pathogen.

Even though Ross' postulations are over two decades old, can you find which attribution you would mostly likely identify with if you were (or have been) diagnosed with an STI? The intention is to decrease the blame on any individual or situation and to help everyone realize that such microorganisms do not discriminate. The negative meanings we place on such a diagnosis decrease the likelihood that individuals will seek screening and treatment, which can lead to serious health complications and exposing others to such infections (Ross, 2008).

REFLECTIONS

The majority of STIs occur in our young adult population. One in four women will be infected with an STI during her lifetime (Garnett, 2008). Given these sobering statistics, and increased openness and awareness, why haven't these infection rates decreased significantly in the past decade? The reasons why individuals have sex, with whom, and with or without protection are extremely complex. Gender power imbalance, lack of comprehensive sexuality education, lack of access or funds to purchase protection, being under the influence of a mind-altering substance—these are just a few reasons why women and men become infected with an STI every year in this country.

CRITICAL THINKING SKILLS

Level 5, Synthesis Compile information together in a different way by combining elements in a new pattern or proposing alternative solutions.

Bloom's Taxonomy Key Words. Develop, discuss, theorize, predict, construct, combine, and elaborate.

CRITICAL THINKING QUESTIONS

1. What ways can you reduce your risk of being infected with an STI?
2. How would you tell a potential sexual partner if you had an incurable STI, such as genital herpes?
3. Would you tell a potential sexual partner that you were once infected with a curable STI, such as chlamydia or gonorrhea? Why or why not?
4. Why do you think it is so difficult to federally mandate all children to get the HPV vaccine, even though there is strong evidence that this can greatly reduce the rate of cancers and genital warts in the cervix, vagina, vulva, penis, anus, and throat?
5. How do you think public policy has helped or hindered your generation from getting the education or the ability to access the resources you need to protect yourselves? How has it helped?

WEBSITES

www.ashastd.org/
American Social Health Association

www.engenderhealth.org
Engender Health

www.popcouncil.org
Population Council

www.who.int/en
World Health Organization (WHO)

REFERENCES

American Social Health Association (2009). HIV and AIDS overview. Retrieved on January 8, 2011, from www.ashastd.org/learn/learn_hiv_aids_overview.cfm, accessed.

American Social Health Association. (1998). *Sexually transmitted diseases in America: How many cases and at what cost?* Research Triangle Park, NC: American Social Health Association.

Bradford, R., Whitley, R., & Stagno, S. (2008). Herpes virus infections in neonates and children: Cytomegalovirus and herpes simplex virus. In K. Holmes, P. Sparling, W. Stamm, P. Piot, J. Wasserheit, L. Corey, & M. Cohen (Eds.), *Sexually Transmitted Diseases*, 4th ed., 1629–1658. New York, NY: McGraw-Hill.

Buve, A., Goubin, C., & Laga, M. (2008). Gender and sexually transmitted diseases. In K. Holmes, P. Sparling, W. Stamm, P. Piot, J. Wasserheit, L. Corey, & M. Cohen (eds.), *Sexually Transmitted Diseases* (4th ed., 151–164). New York, NY: McGraw-Hill.

Cates, W. (2004). Reproductive tract infections. In R. Hatcher, J. Trussell, F. Stewart, A. Nelson, W. Cates, F. Guest, & D. Kowal (eds.), *Contraceptive Technology,* 18th ed., pp. 773–845. New York, NY: Ardent Media.

CDC (2011). *STDs & pregnancy: CDC fact sheet.* Retrieved July 20, 2011, from http://www.cdc.gov/std/pregnancy/STDfact-Pregnancy.htm.

CDC. (2009). Chlamydia screening among sexually active young female enrollees of health plans—United States, 2000–2007, *Morbidity and Mortality Weekly Report, 58*(14), 362–365.

CDC (2008a). *HIV/AIDS in the United States, CDC HIV/AIDS Facts.* www.cdc.gov/hiv/resources/factsheets/us.htm, accessed January 8, 2011.

CDC (2008b). *HIV/AIDS Surveillance Report, 2006.* Atlanta, GA: CDC.

CDC (2008c). New estimates of U.S. HIV prevalence, CDC Fact Sheet, 2006. www.cdc.gov/nchhstp/newsroom/docs/prevalence.pdf, accessed January 8, 2011.

CDC (2008d). *Trends in reportable sexually transmitted diseases in the United States, 2007: National surveillance data for Chlamydia, Gonorrhea, and Syphilis.* Atlanta, GA: CDC.

CDC (2007). Quadrivalent human papillomavirus vaccine: recommendations of the Advisory Committee on Immunization Practices (ACIP). *Morbidity and Mortality Weekly Report,* Vol. 56.

CDC (2002). 2002 guidelines for treatment of sexually transmitted diseases. *Morbidity and Mortality Weekly Report, 51,* 1–80.

Corey, L., & Wald, A. (2008). Genital herpes. In K. Holmes, P. Sparling, W. Stamm, P. Piot, J. Wasserheit, L. Corey, & M. Cohen (Eds.), *Sexually Transmitted Diseases,* 4th ed., 399–438. New York, NY: McGraw-Hill.

Douglas, J. M., Jr. (2009). Penicillin treatment of syphilis: Clearing away the shadow on the land. *Journal of the American Medical Association, 301*(7), 769–771.

Garnett, G. (2008). The transmission dynamics of sexually transmitted infections. In K. Holmes, P. Sparling, W. Stamm, P. Piot, J. Wasserheit, L. Corey, & M. Cohen (eds.), *Sexually Transmitted Diseases,* 4th ed., 27–40. New York, NY: McGraw-Hill.

Geisler, W., & Krieger, J. (2008). Epididymitis. In K. Holmes, P. Sparling, W. Stamm, P. Piot, J. Wasserheit, L. Corey, & M. Cohen (Eds.), *Sexually Transmitted Diseases,* 4th ed., 1127–1146. New York, NY: McGraw-Hill.

Goldenberg, R. L., Andrews, W., Yuan, A., & MacKay, H. T. (1997). Sexually transmitted diseases and adverse outcomes of pregnancy. *Clinics in Perinatology, 24,* 23–41.

Haggerty, C. L., Schulz, R., & Ness, R. B. (2003). Lower quality of life among women with chronic pelvic pain after pelvic inflammatory disease. *Obstetrics & Gynecology, 102,* 934–939.

Hansfield, H. (2008). Principles of treatment of sexually transmitted diseases. In K. Holmes, P. Sparling, W. Stamm, P. Piot, J. Wasserheit, L. Corey, & M. Cohen (Eds.), *Sexually transmitted diseases,* 4th ed., 937–958. New York, NY: McGraw-Hill.

Hillier, S., Marrazzo, J., & Holmes, K. (2008). Bacterial vaginosis. In K. Holmes, P. Sparling, W. Stamm, P. Piot, J. Wasserheit, L. Corey, & M. Cohen (eds.), *Sexually Transmitted Diseases,* 4th ed., 117–127. New York, NY: McGraw-Hill.

Hitti, J., & Watts, H. (2008). Bacterial sexually transmitted infections in pregnancy. In K. Holmes, P. Sparling, W. Stamm, P. Piot, J. Wasserheit, L. Corey, & M. Cohen (eds.), *Sexually Transmitted Diseases,* 4th ed., 1529–1562). New York, NY: McGraw-Hill.

Hook, E., & Handsfield, H. (2008). Gonococcal infection in the adult. In K. Holmes, P. Sparling, W. Stamm, P. Piot, J. Wasserheit, L. Corey, & M. Cohen (eds.), *Sexually Transmitted Diseases,* 4th ed., 627–646. New York, NY: McGraw-Hill.

Jones, R., & Lopez, K. (2006). *Human Reproductive Biology,* 3rd ed. Burlington, MA: Elsevier.

Kohlhoff, S., & Hammerschlag, M. (2008). Gonococcal and chlamydial infections in infants and children. In K. Holmes, P. Sparling, W. Stamm, P. Piot, J. Wasserheit, L. Corey, & M. Cohen (eds.), *Sexually Transmitted Diseases,* 4th ed., 1613–1628. New York, NY: McGraw-Hill.

McGough, L. (2008). Historical perspective on sexually transmitted diseases for prevention and control. In K. Holmes, P. Sparling, W. Stamm, P. Piot, J. Wasserheit, L. Corey, & M. Cohen (Eds.), *Sexually Transmitted Diseases,* 4th ed., 3–12. New York, NY: McGraw-Hill.

Moore, E. A., & Moore, L. M. (2005). *Encyclopedia of sexually transmitted diseases.* Jefferson, NC: McFarland & Company.

Paavonen, J., Westrom, L., & Eschenbach, D. (2008). Pelvic inflammatory disease. In K. Holmes, P. Sparling, W. Stamm, P. Piot, J. Wasserheit, L. Corey, & M. Cohen (eds.), *Sexually Transmitted Diseases,* 4th ed., 1017–1050. New York, NY: McGraw-Hill.

Pertel, P., & Spear, P. (2008). Biology of herpes viruses. In K. Holmes, P. Sparling, W. Stamm, P. Piot, J. Wasserheit, L. Corey, & M. Cohen (eds.), *Sexually Transmitted Diseases,* 4th ed., 381–398. New York, NY: McGraw-Hill.

Rosebury, T. (1971). *Microbes and morals: The strange story of venereal disease.* New York, NY: The Viking Press.

Ross, M. (2008). Psychological perspectives on sexuality and sexually transmitted diseases and HIV infection. In K. Holmes, P. Sparling, W. Stamm, P. Piot, J. Wasserheit, L. Corey, & M. Cohen (eds.), *Sexually Transmitted Diseases,* 4th ed., 137–148. New York, NY: McGraw-Hill.

Ross, M. (1986). *Psychovenereology: Personality and lifestyle factors in sexually transmitted diseases in homosexual men.* New York, NY: Praeger.

Sparling, P., Swartz, M., Musher, D., & Healy, B. (2008). Clinical manifestations of syphilis. In K. Holmes, P. Sparling, W. Stamm, P. Piot, J. Wasserheit, L. Corey, & M. Cohen (eds.), *Sexually Transmitted Diseases*, 4th ed., 661–684. New York, NY: McGraw-Hill.

Stamm, W. (2008). Chlamydia trachomatis infections in the adult. In K. Holmes, P. Sparling, W. Stamm, P. Piot, J. Wasserheit, L. Corey, & M. Cohen (eds.), *Sexually Transmitted Diseases*, 4th ed., 575–594. New York, NY: McGraw-Hill.

Watts, H. (2008). Pregnancy and viral sexually transmitted infections. In K. Holmes, P. Sparling, W. Stamm, P. Piot, J. Wasserheit, L. Corey, & M. Cohen (eds.), *Sexually Transmitted Diseases*, 4th ed., 1563–1576. New York, NY: McGraw-Hill.

Weinstock, H., Berman, S., & Cates, W., Jr. (2004). Sexually transmitted diseases among American youth: incidence and prevalence estimates, 2000. *Perspectives on Sexual & Reproductive Health*, 36(1), 6–10.

Wiesenfeld, H., & Cates, W. (2008). Sexually transmitted diseases and infertility. In K. Holmes, P. Sparling, W. Stamm, P. Piot, J. Wasserheit, L. Corey, & M. Cohen (eds.), *Sexually Transmitted Diseases*, 4th ed., 1511–1528. New York, NY: McGraw-Hill.

Winer, R., & Koutsky, L. (2008). Genital human papillomavirus infection. In K. Holmes, P. Sparling, W. Stamm, P. Piot, J. Wasserheit, L. Corey, & M. Cohen (eds.), *Sexually Transmitted Diseases*, 4th ed., 489–508. New York, NY: McGraw-Hill.

World Health Organization (2005). *Sexually transmitted and other reproductive tract infections: A guide to essential practice*. Geneva, Switzerland: World Health Organization.

CHAPTER

11

1. Discuss the short- and long-term effects of alcohol abuse.
2. Design a concept map indicating the adverse effects of environmental tobacco smoke.
3. Examine the consequences of smoking during pregnancy.
4. Predict the relationship between smoking, cardiovascular disease, and development of respiratory cancer.
5. Apply critical thinking skill Level 4, Analysis.

UNDERSTANDING PROBLEM DRINKING

Why so some people develop problems with alcohol while others do not? The answer points to individual, psychological, and sociocultural factors. A family history of alcoholism can increase one's risk for becoming an alcoholic. Sociocultural or environmental factors can also play a role. Some cultures may have a higher acceptance of alcohol use and abuse, making alcoholism more tolerable. In addition to family history and sociocultural factors, economic factors, such as availability and cost of alcohol, may play a role as well (Teague, Mackenzie, & Rosenthal 2011).

DRINKING AMONG COLLEGE STUDENTS

Research indicates that up to 83 percent of college students drink alcoholic beverages (National Center on Addiction and Substance Abuse, 2007). Some students engage in binge drinking.

Binge Drinking Binge drinking is defined as the consumption of five or more drinks in a row for men and four or more drinks in a row for women at least once the previous two-week period. In 2005, the College Alcohol Study (CAS) conducted by the National Center on Addiction and Substance Use at Columbia University found that about 40 percent of all college students were binge drinkers, and almost one in four were frequent binge drinkers, meaning they had binged three or more times in the previous two weeks or more than once a week on average (Wechsler, et al. 2002).

Binge drinking can cause serious physical, academic, social, and legal problems. Persons who drink heavily are more likely to commit crimes of violence, including homicides or serious assaults (Weitzman & Chen, 2005).

The most serious consequence of binge drinking is alcohol poisoning. Alcohol poisoning results when an overdose of alcohol is consumed. When excessive alcohol is consumed, the brain is deprived of oxygen, which causes the brain to send a message to lungs and heart to slow down functioning. Some symptoms of alcohol poisoning are lack of response to talking, shouting, or being shaken, inability to stand up, slow, labored or abnormal breathing, skin feels clammy, rapid pulse rate, irregular heart rhythm, lowered blood pressure, and vomiting. In case of vomiting, do not leave the person alone. Try to turn the person on her/his side to lessen chance of asphyxiation or choking. Try calling for medical help immediately, and remember, do not leave the person alone.

Who's at Risk? Men binge drink at rates almost three times those of women. Male freshmen drink less than male upperclassmen, while female first-year students drink more than female upperclass students.

Binge drinking rates are similar between racial/ethnic groups. However, non-Hispanic blacks and Hispanics reported a higher number of drinks per binge than whites, and American-born Hispanics report higher binge-drinking rates than foreign-born Hispanics.

Students at historically black colleges and universities (HBCUs) have lower rates of binge drinking than do other college students, perhaps due to family and community expectations, peer modeling, and religion and spirituality implications (Wechsler et al., 2008; Caetano, Ramisetty-Mikler, & Rodriguez, 2008).

ALCOHOL ABSORPTION

There are many factors that affect alcohol absorption, including food in the stomach, gender (women absorb alcohol more quickly than men), mood (if tired or stressed, the stomach empties more rapidly enabling alcohol to be absorbed more easily), and alcohol consumption (the more concentrated the drink, the more quickly alcohol is absorbed).

ALCOHOL METABOLISM

Ninety percent of alcohol is metabolized in the liver and a very small amount is excreted in the breath, skin, and urine.

The liver plays a major role in the metabolism or breaking down of alcohol. An organic chemical substance called alcohol dehydroganese (ADH) is available in the liver. This enzyme does its job quite well, but when there is more alcohol than the liver can process, excess alcohol molecules will circulate to other parts of the body such as the brain and liver until the liver builds up additional ADH to metabolize the alcohol.

Women generally have a higher blood alcohol content than men after drinking the same amount of alcohol. Contributing factors include a higher percentage of body fat and lesser amounts of production of ADH than men.

PHYSIOLOGICAL EFFECTS

Alcohol is a depressant, which means it slows down the central nervous system and cardiovascular system. Alcohol sedates the nervous system. Alcohol also affects the vision by causing the loss of fine muscle control in the eyes that control peripheral vision, color distinction, night vision, and distance judgment. Other effects include impaired mental and physical reflexes and increase risk of cancer of the brain, tongue, mouth, throat, liver, and bladder, as well heart and blood pressure problems.

Alcohol abuse and misuse also contributes to societal problems such as motor vehicles accidents, violence, school problems, and family problems. See Figure 11.1.

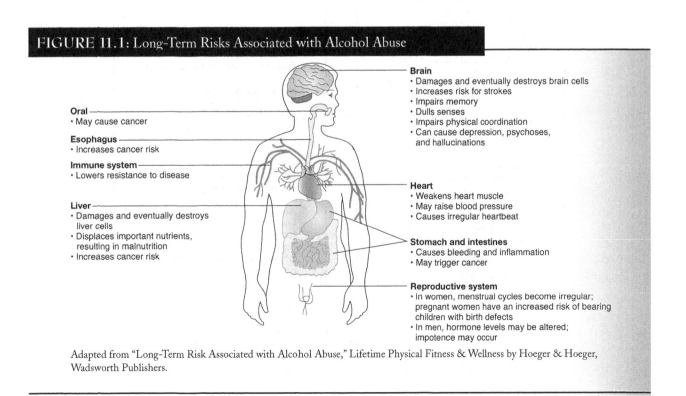

FIGURE 11.1: Long-Term Risks Associated with Alcohol Abuse

Adapted from "Long-Term Risk Associated with Alcohol Abuse," Lifetime Physical Fitness & Wellness by Hoeger & Hoeger, Wadsworth Publishers.

UNDERSTANDING TOBACCO USE

Like alcohol, we are free to abuse and misuse tobacco, but there is a price to be paid. Tobacco use is the leading cause of death in the United States. People who smoke are aware of the health hazards of tobacco use, yet one in five Americans smokes, and nearly 4,000 young people under the age of 18 start smoking everyday (American Lung Association 2007).

TOBACCO PRODUCTS

When tobacco leaves are burned, thousands of substances are produced—among them include 70 that are carcinogenic (cause cancer). Tar, carbon monoxide, and nicotine are the most harmful.

Because tar is a thick, sticky residue, it coats the lungs, increasing the risk of the growth of cancer cells. Carbon monoxide is a hazardous poisoning gas—the same gas that pours out of the exhaust pipe of a car or bus (see Figure 11.2).

FIGURE 11.2: When Smokers Quit

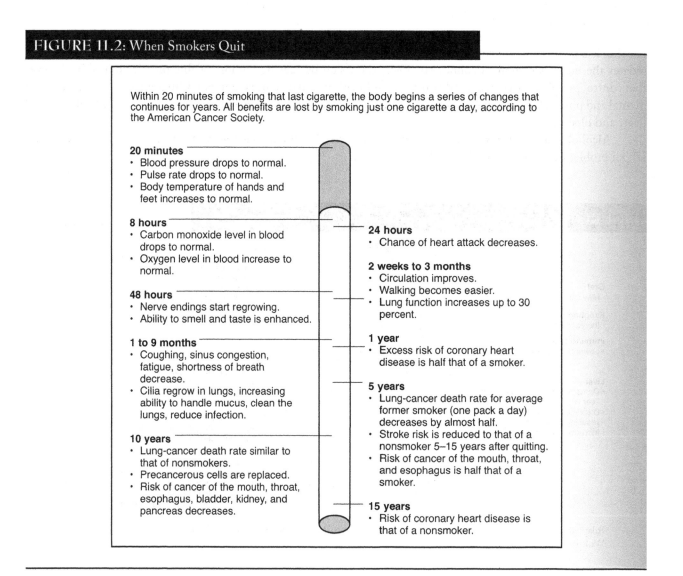

Within 20 minutes of smoking that last cigarette, the body begins a series of changes that continues for years. All benefits are lost by smoking just one cigarette a day, according to the American Cancer Society.

20 minutes
- Blood pressure drops to normal.
- Pulse rate drops to normal.
- Body temperature of hands and feet increases to normal.

8 hours
- Carbon monoxide level in blood drops to normal.
- Oxygen level in blood increase to normal.

48 hours
- Nerve endings start regrowing.
- Ability to smell and taste is enhanced.

1 to 9 months
- Coughing, sinus congestion, fatigue, shortness of breath decrease.
- Cilia regrow in lungs, increasing ability to handle mucus, clean the lungs, reduce infection.

10 years
- Lung-cancer death rate similar to that of nonsmokers.
- Precancerous cells are replaced.
- Risk of cancer of the mouth, throat, esophagus, bladder, kidney, and pancreas decreases.

24 hours
- Chance of heart attack decreases.

2 weeks to 3 months
- Circulation improves.
- Walking becomes easier.
- Lung function increases up to 30 percent.

1 year
- Excess risk of coronary heart disease is half that of a smoker.

5 years
- Lung-cancer death rate for average former smoker (one pack a day) decreases by almost half.
- Stroke risk is reduced to that of a nonsmoker 5–15 years after quitting.
- Risk of cancer of the mouth, throat, and esophagus is half that of a smoker.

15 years
- Risk of coronary heart disease is that of a nonsmoker.

Carbon monoxide and oxygen do not mix well. In fact, carbon monoxide interferes with the ability of the red blood cells to carry oxygen, so that vital organs such as the heart and lungs are not deprived of life-sustaining oxygen. Another harmful ingredient in tobacco is nicotine, a poisonous psychoactive drug that also is used in pesticides. Nicotine is highly addictive, as most smokers can attest. Nicotine is transported into the body in the form of tiny particles that are suspended in partially burned tobacco. These droplets are so tiny that they are capable of penetrating the small air sacs in the lungs and enter the blood stream with ease.

Which Is More Harmful: Cigarettes or Cigars? Cigars are more harmful than cigarettes. Why? Cigars have more tobacco and nicotine per unit than cigarettes. Cigars take longer to smoke, generate more smoke, and have more combustion products than cigarettes. The tobacco mix used in cigars makes it easier for cigar smoke to be absorbed through the mucous membranes of the oral cavity than is the case with cigarettes.

Cigar smokers who do not inhale have lower mortality rates than cigar smokers who do (Wechsler et al. 2001).

SHORT-TERM EFFECTS

Nicotine is such a powerful drug that it affects every system in the body.. Nicotine particles reach the brain within 7 to 10 seconds, causing a relaxing effect. The heart rate and blood pressure increases 10 to 20 beats and 5 to 10 points, respectively (Levington 2003).

The tar and poisons in tobacco when burned damage cilia, the hairlike structures in the bronchial passages that prevent toxins and debris from reaching the lung tissue.

Carbon monoxide in tobacco smoke affects the way smokers process the air they breathe. Here's how. Oxygen is carried through the bloodstream by hemoglobin, a protein in red blood cells. However, when carbon monoxide is present, the carbon monoxide binds with red blood cells, preventing red blood cells from carrying the amount of oxygen blood normally carries. As a result, heavy smokers quickly become winded during physical activity such as climbing steps, running, and fast-paced walking. More importantly, the cardiovascular system breaks down in that it cannot effectively deliver oxygen to muscle cells (Krogh 1999).

LONG-TERM EFFECTS

Cardiovascular disease, cancer, and respiratory diseases are the major health concerns associated with smoking. Nicotine can make blood platelets stickier, leading to hypertension, heart attack, stroke, and other forms of heart disease (United States Department of Health and Human Services 2004). People who smoke more than one pack of cigarettes per day have three times the risk for heart disease and congestive heart failure that nonsmokers have (Goren & Schnoll 2006).

Thirty percent of all cancers that affect the pancreas, kidney, bladder, breast, and cervix are associated with smoking. Smoking and using tobacco also play a major role in cancers of the mouth, throat, and esophagus. Oral cancers caused by smokeless tobacco tend to occur early in adulthood. Alcohol use combined with tobacco increases the risk of oral cancers (National Cancer Institute, n.d).

Other health effects caused by smoking include pulmonary diseases such as emphysema, an abnormal condition of the lungs in which the air sacs in the lungs become enlarged and lose their elasticity, making it difficult to breathe (see Figure 11.3). In addition, bronchitis and asthma are also serious tobacco-induced health problems that can seriously compromise individual's quality of life (United States Department of Health and Human Services 2004).

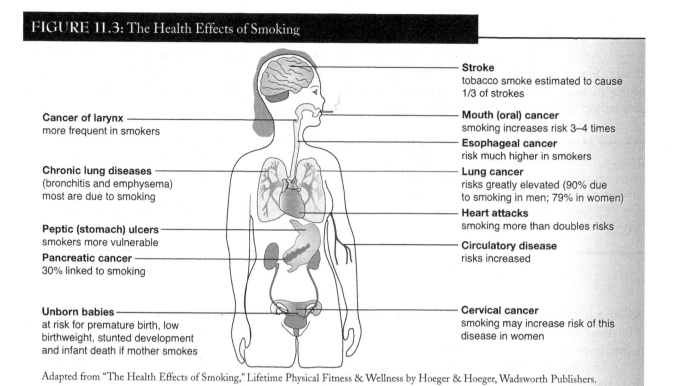

Stroke
tobacco smoke estimated to cause
1/3 of strokes

Mouth (oral) cancer
smoking increases risk 3–4 times

Esophageal cancer
risk much higher in smokers

Lung cancer
risks greatly elevated (90% due
to smoking in men; 79% in women)

Heart attacks
smoking more than doubles risks

Circulatory disease
risks increased

Cervical cancer
smoking may increase risk of this
disease in women

Cancer of larynx
more frequent in smokers

Chronic lung diseases
(bronchitis and emphysema)
most are due to smoking

Peptic (stomach) ulcers
smokers more vulnerable

Pancreatic cancer
30% linked to smoking

Unborn babies
at risk for premature birth, low
birthweight, stunted development
and infant death if mother smokes

Adapted from "The Health Effects of Smoking," Lifetime Physical Fitness & Wellness by Hoeger & Hoeger, Wadsworth Publishers.

SECONDHAND SMOKE

Are people who breathe mainstream smoke at risk for similar health problems? Inhaling the smoke from other people's tobacco products for as little as 30 minutes a day causes heart damage. People who are exposed daily to secondhand smoke have a 30 percent higher rate of death and disease than nonsmokers who are not exposed (Payne, Hahn, & Lucas 2006).

INTERVENTION: AN EFFORT TO STOP WHAT YOU STARTED

Before people will discontinue harmful health behaviors, such as tobacco and alcohol use, they must understand what to expect of themselves. Having knowledge about the health risks associated with substance abuse, familiarity with steps that can be taken to reduce or eliminate risks, knowledge of benefits gained, and motivation to stop using tobacco or alcohol will certainly increase one's chances of being successful at quitting. Even if individuals relapse, continual efforts to quit are worthwhile.

REFLECTION

Tobacco and alcohol abuse are two of the most preventable causes of death. Although some tobacco companies refute the dangers of smoking, millions of Americans die each year of tobacco-related diseases, with alcohol-related fatalities close behind. The best prevention from tobacco- and alcohol-related diseases is to abstain from excessive drinking and quit smoking.

CRITICAL THINKING SKILL

Level 4, Analysis. Examine and break information into parts by identifying motives or cause. Make inferences and find evidence to support generalizations.

Bloom's Taxonomy Key Words. Compare and contrast, list, relationships, examine, distinguish, predict, breakdown, outline, and analyze.

CRITICAL THINKING QUESTIONS

1. Compare and contrast the effects of alcohol and tobacco use.
2. Draw a diagram indicating your negative and positive (if you don't use tobacco or alcohol) risks for developing adverse health conditions for tobacco and/or alcohol use.
3. Does anyone ever recover from alcoholism? Explain.

WEBSITES

www.factsontap.org

This excellent site is geared to college students. Sections include Alcohol & Student life, Alcohol & Your Body.

www.nacoa.org

The National Association for Children of Alcoholics provides information and referrals to local Al-Anon and Alateen groups. It also includes a self-quiz to determine if you are affected by someone who has an alcohol problem.

www.tobacco.neu.edu

The site provides current information on tobacco-related litigation and legislature.

www.lungsusa.org

This American Lung Association site provides access to many facts and resources regarding tobacco use.

REFERENCES

American Lung Association. (2007). Smoking and teens fact sheet. www.lungusa.org/site/pp.asp?c=dvLUK9O0E &b=39871.

Caetano, R., Ramisetty-Mikler, S., & Rodriguez, L. A. (2008). The Hispanic Americans baseline alcohol survey: DUI rates, birthplace, and acculturation across Hispanic national groups. *Journal of Studies of Alcohol, 69* (2), 159–265.

Goren, S. S., & Schnoll, R. A. (2006). Smoking cessation. In S. S. Goren & J. Arnold (eds.), *Health promotion in practice*. San Francisco: Jossey-Bass.

Krogh, D. (1999). *Smoking: The artificial passion.* New York: W. H. Freeman and Company.

Levington, S. (2003). The importance of cholesterol, blood pressure, and smoking for coronary heart disease. *European Heart Journal, 24* (19), 1703–1704.

National Cancer Institute. (n.d). Fact Sheet: Cigarette smoking and cancer: Questions and answers, www.cancer.gov/cancertopics/factsheet/tobacco/cancer.

National Center on Addiction and Substance Abuse. (2007). *Wasting the best and the brightest: Substance abuse at American's colleges and universities.* New York: Columbia University.

Payne, W., Hahn, D., & Lucas, E. (2006). *Focus on Health* (9th ed.). Boston: McGraw-Hill.

Teague, M., Mackenzie, S., & Rosenthal, D. (2011). *Your health.* New York: McGraw-Hill, Inc.

United States Department of Health and Human Services. (2004). The health consequences of smoking: *A report of the surgeon general.* Atlanta: Author.

Wechsker, H., & Nelson, T. (2008). What we have learned from Harvard School of Public Health College Alcohol Study: Focusing attention on college student alcohol consumption and environmental conditions that promote it. *Journal of Studies of Alcohol, 69* (3), 481–489.

Wechsler, H., Lee, J. E., Nelson, T. F., & Kuo, M. (2002). Underage college students: Drinking behavior, access to alcohol, and the influence of deterrence policies. Findings from the Harvard School of Public Health College Study. *Journal of American College Health, 50* (5), 223–236.

Wechsler, H., Lee, J. E., Nelson, T. F., & Lee, H. (2001). Drinking levels, alcohol problems, and second-hand effects in substance-free colleges residences: Results of a national study. *Journal of Studies on Alcohol, 62* (1), 23–31.

Weitzman, E., & Chen, Y. (2005). Risk modifying effect of social capital on heavy alcohol consumption, alcohol abuse, harms, and secondhand effects: National survey findings. *Journal of Epidemiology, 59* (4), 303–309.

CHAPTER

12

Illicit Drug Use, Misuse, and Abuse

1. Define addiction.
2. Discuss the signs of addiction.
3. Discuss the stages of addiction.
4. Describe types of psychoactive drugs and the effects they have on the body.
5. Apply critical thinking skills Level 5 and 6, Synthesis and Evaluation.

ADDICTIVE BEHAVIOR

Addiction is a process, much like a journey. Process involves movement, development, and change. As an addiction develops, it becomes a way of life that's continually changing. As mentioned earlier, addiction is defined as the continued use of a chemical or continual participation in a behavior despite negative consequences. The stages of addiction indicate a process—an addictive journey.

Addiction is the continued involvement with a substance or activity despite ongoing negative consequences. Addictive behavior includes addictions to shopping, sex, gambling, food, television, videogames, work, and Internet use. Signs of addiction have four common aspects: compulsion/obsession, loss of control, negative consequences, and denial:

1. *Compulsion* is distinguished by obsession or excessive preoccupation with the behavior and the overwhelming need to perform it.
2. *Loss of control* or inability to predict whether any isolated occurrence of the behavior will be healthy or damaging.
3. *Negative consequences,* such as physical damage, legal trouble, financial problems, academic failure, and family dissolution, which do not occur with healthy involvement in any behavior.
4. *Denial* is the inability to perceive the self-destructive nature of the addiction. These four components are present in all addictions, whether chemical or behavioral addictions (Donatelle 2010).

STAGE ONE: INTERNAL CHANGE

Many changes take place within the addict before anyone suspects or knows there is a problem. In stage one, the addicts' personality will alter permanently. When the addict first experiences the high, the journey starts. The mood changes that addicts experience at the onset are very enjoyable and intense. During this initial stage, the addict turns to natural relationships (e.g., family members) or support, nurturing, guidance, love, and emotional and spiritual support.

There is also a period in time when the addict seeks an illusion of relief to avoid unpleasant feelings or situations. This is nurturing through avoidance—an unnatural way of taking care of one's emotional needs. Consequently, many times the addict will give up natural relationships and replace them with addictive relationships, which is the beginning of the addictive cycle. The addictive cycle is depicted as a downward spiral with many valleys and plateaus (Nakken 1996).

By accepting and taking responsibility for her/his dual personality, the addict can begin the road to recovery. With understanding and listening to the addictive logic, the addict can enter a recovery program being totally honest with one's self.

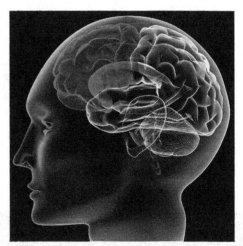

© 2011 by YAKOBCHUK VASYL. Used under license of Shutterstock, Inc.

STAGE TWO: LIFESTYLE CHANGE

Since the addict's behavior is the most visible part of the addiction and the easiest to focus attention on, behaviors such as bingeing on and purging food, compulsively going to porn shops, overspending, or compulsive chemical abuse are clearly seen by others as out of control.

In stage two, addicts start to arrange their lives and relationships using addictive logic. For example, the decision to gravitate to other addicts for nurturing, love is a common addictive strategy used by addicts to justify their desire to reinforce addictive behavior. In this stage the commitment to the addictive process has become all-encompassing. Consequently, the person starts to lie, almost about everything, blames others, knowing others are not to blame, and withdraws from others. Food addicts may start hiding food or starving themselves; sex addicts may start going to prostitutes or have multiple affairs; alcoholics may begin to have a couple of quick shots and a few breath mints before going home.

To make sense of their own behavior, addicts will deny the physical consequences of their behavior as well as emotional pain caused by their inappropriate behavior (Nakken 1996).

STAGE THREE: LIFE BREAKDOWN

In this stage, the addict's life literally starts to break down under the tremendous stress, pain, and fear that is a consequence of his or her behavior. Although acting out behavior caused by drug abuse, compulsive food, gambling, or sex behavior still produces a mood change, the pain and fear are too intense for the addict to ignore any longer. The excuses that made logical sense are now questionable. Addictive coping strategies work against the addictive process, causing the addict to see her/him self in a different light—a pitiful, weak, destructive individual.

Despite all the personal discomforts, the addict cannot break the cycle alone. Unless help or an intervention occurs, the addict will stay stuck in stage three. To recover, the addict must learn how to reach out, to connect with others. In doing so, addicts can discover a new way of coping with life (Nakken 1996).

RISK FACTORS FOR ADDICTION

Addiction is caused by a variety of biological, psychological, and environmental factors. Biological factors may include early substance use as well as use of drugs for biological disorders such as depression and bipolar disorders. Psychological factors including low self-esteem, and post-traumatic stress disorders as well as stressful life events can increase one's risk for addiction. Moreover, having easy access to drugs, residing in an abusive or neglectful home environment, and/or being a part of a marginalized group can also increase one's risk for addiction.

DYSFUNCTIONAL FAMILY RULES: DON'T TALK, DON'T TRUST, DON'T FEEL

Children who are raised in addictive homes experience depression and a sense of emptiness, which makes it difficult to maintain intimate close relationships. Because life appears meaningless, their compulsive behaviors such as work, spending or gambling, or food disorders become an important part of their life. To break the cycle, children of addictive parents must recognize the process that has occurred.

DON'T TALK

Rationalizing the addictive behavior is "normal" behavior for families dealing with addiction. In most addictive families, the rule is to say nothing. To acknowledge the addicts' inappropriate behavior is to admit that something is wrong, and admitting that something or someone is wrong disturbs the "normal" way of life. Consequently, family members find it easier to do and say nothing for fear of losing control.

DON'T TRUST

Children raised in addictive families learn that it is not safe to trust others with their personal problems. To trust means to let one's guard down in order to have confidence and faith in another person. When family members play a role in embarrassing and humiliating children, it is difficult to trust those members of the family and others outside the family. Furthermore, when family members deny the events that caused hurt and humiliation, children raised in addictive homes are left feeling insecure and unsafe.

DON'T FEEL

Like the addict, children of addicts have many feelings to contend with such as fear of abandonment and violence; guilt due to self-blame; sadness over the many losses; anger about repeated broken promises; and embarrassment over addictive parents' behavior. By detaching from others, children raised in addictive families learn not to feel or share feelings with others.

OTHER DYSFUNCTIONAL RULES

Children raised in addictive families also adhere to other rules that become a part of their lives, such as *don't play*. The consequence of playing is not being around adults, whose behavior dictates what is going to happen next. *Don't make a mistake* is another rule that most children who are raised in addictive homes learn to adhere to at an early age. As a result, adult children of addicts may develop a need to be perfect in every way (Black 2001).

When all these rules are applied, it is no wonder that a child who feels lost and alone will develop roles that help them and other family members cope with the addiction.

HOW ADDICTION AFFECTS FAMILY MEMBERS

Family members and friends of an addicted person can show signs of addiction as well as the addicted person. Many times, family members in their need to help the addict struggle with codependence, which is an unhealthy self-defeating emotional relationship with the addict that can lead to family and friends knowingly or unknowingly protecting the addict from the natural consequences of their behavior.

Enablers usually make excuses for the addict's negative behavior, which only serves to reinforce the addict's addiction and family members' codependence. Children raised in addictive homes will find ways to survive in an environment that promotes dysfunction by moving into various role patterns.

THE RESPONSIBLE CHILD

Usually the oldest child carries a lot of responsibility for the caring and nurturing of siblings in the family. As a child, this person has learned to take control, set realistic goals, and make adult decisions. During their teen years, children who assume the responsible role are so busy as adults that they spent little or no time experiencing what it is like to be a child. For the responsible child, intimate relationships are too uncomfortable to maintain (Black 2001).

THE ADJUSTER

Adult adjusters find it easier to avoid situations where they need to take control. They function at taking life in stride (Black 2001). In fact, adapting to life's circumstances in this manner becomes a source of pride. Adjusters do not have time to trust on an ongoing basis, nor are they able to develop healthy relationships. Based on this behavior pattern, no wonder adjusters find mates who are contentious (Black 2001).

THE PLACATER

The placater is a warm, caring and sensitive person who sometimes jest or make light of the situation to make others feel better. Placaters have difficulty looking out for their needs, and prefer to satisfy the needs of others. Although this behavior appears to be healthy on the surface, the placater still feels apart from others and thus looks for people who don't want personal sharing from a friend or loved one (Black 2001).

ACTING-OUT CHILD

The acting-out child or the scapegoat is one who constantly finds trouble and causes problems. In fact, as both children and adults, the acting-out child has a propensity for trouble, which can cause major problems. The acting-out child may share the placater's sense of humor and creativity (Black 2001).

Despite the deficits found in each of the four roles mentioned, children raised in addictive homes have strengths and capabilities that have not been explored or applied. Similar to the addict, interventions requiring movement away from self is one step toward the recovery process.

PSYCHOACTIVE DRUGS

Psychoactive drugs are illicit or legal drugs that account for one in five females and one in three males becoming addicted (Floyd, Mimms, & Yelding, 2008). Psychoactive drugs contain substances that have the ability to alter the normal functioning of the body and mind.

According to Floyd, Mimms, and Yelding (2008), illicit drugs are classified as illegal because of their damaging effects, which may include the following:
- Drug dependency
- Physical and mental dysfunctioning
- Disruption of the family unit
- Criminal and destructive behavior
- Premature and accidental death
- Disruption of career goals and aspirations
- Incarceration

STIMULANTS

Cocaine/Crack Cocaine is a white powder that enters the body in a matter of seconds or minutes, depending on the route of administration. Cocaine can be snorted, injected intravenously, or mixed with heroin. When mixed with heroin, it is referred to as speedballing. While the user experiences an intense rush, the euphoria only lasts a few minutes, after which the user crashes.

Crack cocaine is a rock-like crystalline form of cocaine made by combining hydrochloride with common baking soda. In its rock form, crack cocaine can be heated in a pipe, enabling the vapors to be inhaled into the lungs. The high form of crack is short-lived and costly. A single dose of crack sells for approximately $30. To maintain a frequent supply, addicts will often resort to stealing, prostitution, or dealing drugs in order to "feed" their habit.

© 2011 by Anja Peternelj. Used under license of Shutterstock, Inc.

To counter feelings of dysphoria, the user takes another dose within a short period of time. Adverse effects include rapid heartbeat that could lead to heart tachycardia, which can cause the heart to stop beating. Cocaine use can also cause the blood pressure to rise, possibly causing stroke as well as insomnia, irritability, mood swings, paranoia, and depression.

Amphetamines Amphetamines stimulate the body's production of adrenaline hormone and norepinephrine. These two hormones affect the portion of the brain that controls breathing, heart rhythm, blood pressure, and metabolic rate. Amphetamines act directly on the central nervous system causing a sense of well-being, wakefulness, confidence, excitement, and talkativeness. Most users take amphetamines in capsule form called uppers, bennies, dexies, and jolly beans.

Methamphetamines Methamphetamines, commonly referred to as meth, speed, crystal, chalk, ice, glass, bantu, and crank, is one of the most dangerous drugs in the United States. Methamphetamine is usually smoked in a glass pipe or injected, causing intense euphoria, sometimes followed by nausea and vomiting. Continued use can result in aggressive and violent behavior, paranoia, weight loss, kidney and lung failure, cardiovascular disorders, and possible death.

Caffeine Caffeine is an alkaloid substance found in coffee, tea, cola, and chocolate, as well as some prescription drugs and medications. Caffeine levels peak in the body within an hour of consumption, and more than half of the caffeine is broken down in three to seven hours. The stimulant nature of the caffeine causes a feeling of well-being and alertness. Taken in larger doses, caffeine can also contribute to faster heartbeat, irregular heartbeat, extreme nervousness, irritability, ringing in the ears, and insomnia.

Marijuana There are several hundred chemicals in marijuana that are linked to lung cancer and cause damage to the immune and reproductive system. Like all psychoactive drugs, marijuana is also a mind-altering drug that affects each user differently. Despite experiencing physical changes, marijuana users usually experience food cravings, a relaxed mood, heightened sensitivity to music, impairment of short-term memory, overestimation of the passage of time, and loss of ability to maintain attention to the task at hand.

DEPRESSANTS

Depressants are sedatives that depress the central nervous system, reducing or relieving tension and inducing relaxation or sleep. Depressants are powerful drugs capable of producing dependency within two to four weeks. Common physiological effects include drowsiness, impaired judgment, poor coordination, confusion, weak and rapid heartbeat, and pain relief.

Barbiturates Barbiturates also induce relaxation, sleep, and relieve tension, and are usually taken in pill or liquid form. There are two types of barbiturates, short and long acting. Short-acting barbiturates are absorbed rapidly into the brain, while long-acting barbiturates are absorbed slowly into the blood stream.

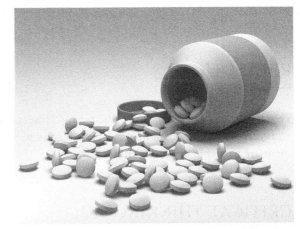

© 2011 by Malashevska Olena. Used under license of Shutterstock, Inc.

NARCOTICS

Narcotics are drugs that relieve pain and often induce sleep. Opium, morphine, codeine, and heroin fall into this category of drugs. Morphine is ten times stronger than opium and is commonly used to relieve pain in drug addicts who are trying to stay clean from heroin or cocaine use, as well as in postoperative patients.

Heroin is a fast-acting pain killer that is usually injected beneath the skin's surface. Overdose of heroin can cause death instantly. Withdrawal symptoms occur within four to six hours after injection. Full-blown withdrawal symptoms include uncontrollable shaking, sweating, chills, vomiting, abdominal pains, and diarrhea.

CLUB DRUGS

Ecstasy, rohypnol, gamma hydroxybutyrate (GHB), 2C-B, and katamine hydrochloride fall into this category of drugs. Drugs that are not easily detected in food and drink are popular club scene drugs. Club drugs are also referred to as *date rape* drugs because individuals who are given the drugs without their knowledge are unable to resist sexual assault. Club drugs, usually in tablet form, produce sedative effects, including muscle relaxation, dizziness, and memory loss.

ANABOLIC STEROIDS

Anabolic steroids are manmade and very similar to male sex hormones. The word anabolic means muscle building. It is illegal for individuals to use steroids to increase muscle mass or enhance physical performance. Steroids can be administered in creams or gels or can be taken orally or injected.

Consequences from steroid use can cause serious health concerns, such as problems with normal hormone production, cardiovascular disease, high blood

© 2011 by Ana Blazic. Used under license of Shutterstock, Inc.

pressure, sleeplessness, and stroke because steroids increase levels of LDL (bad cholesterol) while decreasing HDL (good cholesterol). There can also be liver damage, muscular and ligament damage, as well as stunted bone growth. In females, steroid use can cause facial hair growth and the cessation of the menstrual cycle (Donatelle 2010).

REFLECTION

People from all walks of life use illicit drugs. The misuse and abuse of drugs is on the rise, particularly among teens and college students. Children raised in an addictive environments are also at risk, but timely intervention and treatment are available to anyone in need.

CRITICAL THINKING SKILLS

Level 5, Synthesis Compile information together in a different way by combining elements in a new pattern or proposing alternative solutions.

Bloom's Taxonomy Key Words. Develop, discuss, theorize, predict, construct, combine, and elaborate.

CRITICAL THINKING QUESTIONS FOR LEVEL 5, SYNTHESIS

1. Develop a treatment plan for addiction using the signs of addiction and including the stages of addiction.
2. Discuss how addiction affects the family.
3. If you come from an addictive family or know an addictive friend, describe the type of addiction, your or your friend's signs of the addiction, examples of the addictive behavior, and your or your friend's stage of addiction.

CRITICAL THINKING SKILLS

Level 6, Evaluation Present and defend opinions by making judgments about information, validity of ideas, or quality of work based on a set of criteria.

Bloom's Taxonomy Key Words. Evaluation: determine, defend, support, explain, conclude, evaluate, rate, and prioritize.

CRITICAL THINKING QUESTIONS FOR LEVEL 6, EVALUATION

1. Evaluate the greater risk: tobacco or alcohol. Additional research is required to support your position.
2. Make a list of priorities of importance that influence your decision to not use drugs or to quit using drugs.

WEBSITES

www.well.com/user/woa

This site has a wealth of information about various addictions.

www.jointogether.org

Information on the latest statistics and findings in drug research.

REFERENCES

Black, C. (2001). *It will never happen to me*. Bainbridge Island, WA: MAC Publishing.

Donatelle, R. (2010). *Access to health*. San Francisco: Pearson Benjamin Cummings.

Floyd, P., Mimms, S., & Yelding, C. (2008). *Personal health: Perspectives and lifestyles*. Belmont, CA: Thomson Wadsworth.

Nakken, C. (1996). *The addictive personality*. Center City, MN: Hazelden

CHAPTER

13

Cancer

WHAT IS CANCER?

The American Cancer Society (2011) defines *cancer* as a group of diseases characterized by uncontrolled growth and spread. Other terms you should know related to cancer are: *tumor,* a neoplasmic mass that grows more rapidly than surrounding tissue; *benign,* identified as harmless (refers to a non-cancerous tumor); *malignant* (identified as harmful—refers to a cancerous tumor); *in situ* (noninvasive), having cancer cells present only in the layer of cells where they developed and have not spread; and *invasive,* having cancer cells penetrate the original layer of tissue.

© 2011 by Mark Poprocki. Used under license of Shutterstock, Inc.

All cancers involve the breakdown of genes that control cell growth and division (DeVita, Lawrence, & Rosenberg, 2008). The development of normal human cells mostly depends on the information contained in the cells' chromosomes. Chromosomes are large molecules of deoxyribonucleic acid or DNA. DNA is the chemical that carries the instructions for nearly everything cells do. Some genes (packets of DNA) have instructions for controlling when cells grow and divide. Certain genes that promote cell division are called *oncogenes*. Others that slow down cell division or cause cells to die at the right time are called *tumor suppressor genes.*

Cancers can be caused by DNA mutations (gene defects) that turn on oncogenes or turn off tumor suppressor genes (DeVita, Lawrence, & Rosenberg, 2008). For example, the human papillomavirus (HPV) causes the production of two proteins known as E6 and E7 (Martin & Gutkind, 2009). When these proteins are produced, they turn off some tumor suppressor genes. This may allow cells to grow uncontrollably, which in some cases will lead to cancer. HPV is considered the most common sexually transmitted infection that is responsible for more than half a million new cases annually of cancer worldwide, including those of the cervix, anus, vulva, penis, and of the head and neck area and oral cavity (zur Hausen, 2009).

Exposure to certain external factors, such as tobacco or certain infectious organisms (e.g., HPV) can lead to cancer. The timeframe from external exposure and a cancer diagnosis is 10 years or more (ACS, 2011). Internal factors such as heritance can also increase one's risk to cancer. Cancer is considered a non-communicable disease—it is not transmitted from person to person. For many cancers, prevention is the key for the number of diagnosis and deaths to decrease substantially in the United States (and around the world). Many people are unaware that our behaviors *now* can affect our health decades in our future. Prevention starts today for a healthy tomorrow!

CANCER STATISTICS

Cancer is the second leading cause of death in the United States, surpassed only by cardiovascular disease. The American Cancer Society (2011) estimates 1,529,560 new cancer cases were diagnosed in the United States in

2011. People treated for any noninvasive cancer, as well as basal and squamous cell skin cancer, were not included in the estimate given above because reporting or inclusion of these cancers were not required. The top five states with the leading new cancer cases in 2011 were California, Florida, New York, Texas, and Pennsylvania.

The leading cancer diagnosed in men in the United States in 2011 was prostate cancer. The leading cancer diagnosed in women in the United States in 2011 was breast cancer. Neither of these cancers, though, was the leading cancer for deaths in 2011. That "honor" went to lung cancer for both women and men (ACS, 2011).

CANCER IN MEN (DIAGNOSIS)

The American Cancer Society (2011) estimates 822,300 new cases of cancer occurred in men in 2011. The top ten cancers diagnosed in men are listed as follows:

1. Prostate (29%)
2. Lung & bronchus (14%)
3. Colon & rectum (9%)
4. Urinary bladder (6%)
5. Melanoma of the skin (5%)
6. Kidney & renal pelvis (5%)
7. Non-Hodgkin lymphoma (4%)
8. Oral cavity & pharynx (3%)
9. Leukemia (3%)
10. Pancreas (3%)

Cancer in the Prostate Gland
© 2011 by Sebastian Kaulitzki. Used under license of Shutterstock, Inc.

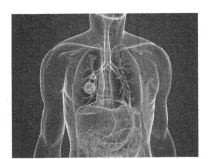

Cancer in the Lungs
© 2011 by Sebastian Kaulitzki. Used under license of Shutterstock, Inc.

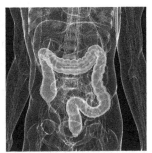

Cancer in the Colon
© 2011 by Sebastian Kaulitzki. Used under license of Shutterstock, Inc.

CANCER IN WOMEN (DIAGNOSIS)

The American Cancer Society (2011) estimates 774,370 new cancer cases occurred in women in 2011. The top ten cancers diagnosed in women are listed as follows:

1. Breast (30%)
2. Lung & bronchus (14%)
3. Colon & rectum (9%)
4. Uterine corpus (6%)
5. Thyroid (5%)
6. Non-Hodgkin lymphoma (4%)
7. Melanoma of the skin (4%)
8. Kidney & renal pelvis (3%)
9. Ovary (3%)
10. Pancreas (3%)

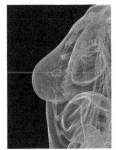

Cancer in the Breast
© 2011 by Sebastian Kaulitzki. Used under license of Shutterstock, Inc.

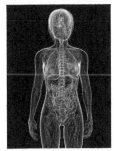

Cancer in the Lungs
© 2011 by Sebastian Kaulitzki. Used under license of Shutterstock, Inc.

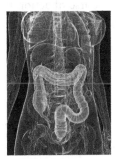

Cancer in the Colon
© 2011 by Sebastian Kaulitzki. Used under license of Shutterstock, Inc.

Compare the leading cancers diagnosed in women and men and identify which cancers are more likely to occur in men than in women and vice versa. Excluding cancers specific to a particular sex (i.e., men can't be diagnosed with ovarian cancer because they do not have ovaries), why do you think some cancers occur in one sex over the other? Which cancers seem to occur almost equally in both women and men? Why do you think that's the case?

CANCER IN MEN (DEATHS)

The American Cancer Society (2011) estimates 300,430 deaths due to cancer occurred in men in 2011. The top ten cancers that resulted in death in men are listed as follows:

1. Lung & bronchus (28%)
2. Prostate (11%)
3. Colon & rectum (8%)
4. Pancreas (6%)
5. Liver and Intrahepatic bile duct (4%)
6. Leukemia (4%)
7. Esophagus (4%)
8. Urinary bladder (4%)
9. Non-Hodgkin lymphoma (3%)
10. Kidney & renal pelvis (3%)

CANCER IN WOMEN (DEATHS)

The American Cancer Society (2011) estimates 271,520 deaths due to cancer occurred in women in 2011. The top ten cancers that resulted in death in women are listed as follows:

1. Lung & bronchus (26%)
2. Breast (15%)
3. Colon & rectum (9%)
4. Pancreas (7%)
5. Ovary (6%)
6. Non-Hodgkin lymphoma (4%)
7. Leukemia (3%)
8. Uterine corpus (3%)
9. Liver and Intrahepatic bile duct (2%)
10. Brain and other nervous system (2%)

© 2011, American Cancer Society, Inc., Surveillance Research.

Compare the leading cancers that resulted in deaths in women and men and identify which cancers are more likely to occur in men than in women and vice versa. What cancers appeared in the list of leading cancers that resulted in deaths, but not in the list of leading cancers diagnosed? Were there noticeable differences when comparing women and men?

STAGING SYSTEM FOR CANCER

Staging describes the extent or spread of the cancer at the time of diagnosis. A cancer's stage is based on the primary tumor's size and whether it has spread to other areas of the body (ACS, 2011). Staging the cancer helps identify the best course of action to take in preventing the spread of the disease, as well as improving quality of life. The four stages are described as follows:

STAGE I

- The cancer is localized.
- The tumor is small in size (1–2 cm, which is around the size of a single pea or a single peanut, respectively).
- The cancer hasn't spread to the lymph nodes.

STAGE II

- The tumor is small in size, but it has spread to the lymph nodes.
- The tumor is larger in size (3–4 cm, which is around the size of a single strawberry or a walnut, respectively), but it hasn't spread to the lymph nodes.

STAGE III

- The tumor is larger than 5 cm (which is around the size of a single lime).

STAGE IV

- The tumor has spread to other parts of the body.

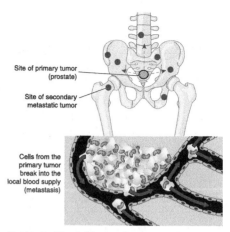

Site of primary tumor
(prostate)

Site of secondary
metastatic tumor

Cells from the
primary tumor
break into the
local blood supply
(metastasis)

© 2011 by Blamb. Used under license of
Shutterstock, Inc.

PREVENTION

PRIMARY PREVENTION

Primary prevention of cancer means an individual does not place her or himself at risk of factors that are known to cause cancer. There is strong evidence to suggest that certain cancers are completely preventable if healthy behaviors are adopted permanently. For example, the American Cancer Society (2011) reports that all the cancers caused by cigarette smoking and heavy alcohol use could have been avoided if our society abstained from tobacco use and promoted, encouraged, and supported drinking alcohol in moderation (if at all).

© 2011 by svand. Used under license of Shutterstock, Inc.

© 2011 by Gts. Used under license of Shutterstock, Inc.

Moreover, cancers related to overweight or obesity, physical inactivity, and poor nutrition could be prevented if society promoted, encouraged, and supported healthy weight maintenance, daily exercise, and consumption of high nutrient-dense foods. Certain cancers related to infectious organisms, such as HPV, hepatitis B virus (HBV), and human immunodeficiency virus (HIV), could decrease significantly (more) if society promoted, encouraged, and supported sexual abstinence, access to reliable barrier contraceptive methods, comprehensive sexuality education, and access to vaccines. Lastly, the majority of skin cancers could be averted if society promoted, encouraged, and supported appropriate clothing when outdoors, application of sunscreen, reduction in tanning salon usage, and yearly skin checkups.

SECONDARY PREVENTION

Secondary prevention of cancer means a person is screened to attempt to diagnose and treat abnormal cells in its early stages before a tumor is formed, progresses in size, or has spread to other organs. Cancers of the cervix, colon, and rectum can be prevented if precancerous cells are detected and removed during the initial stage of the disease (ACS, 2011). Cancers of the breast, cervix, colon, oral cavity, prostate gland, rectum, and skin can be diagnosed early through screening. For individuals with fair skin, for instance, this would mean a yearly skin checkup with a dermatologist. People should check their skin regularly, though, for any unusual moles, new moles, or moles that have grown in size or changed in color and report such changes to their doctor for prompt treatment. At least half of all new cancer cases in 2011 could have been prevented or detected earlier if screening and treatment had been provided (ACS, 2011).

TERTIARY PREVENTION

Tertiary prevention of cancer aims to reduce the negative impact of this established disease by restoring function and reducing disease-related complications. Usually, the goal is to prevent the tumor from growing or spreading to other areas of the body (especially vital organs). Thus, treatment may involve surgical removal of the tumor; surgical removal of a particular body part affected (such as the breast or the prostate gland); radiation therapy (using high-energy radiation to shrink tumors and destroy cancer cells); chemotherapy (anticancer drugs); and hormone therapy (DeVita, Lawrence, & Rosenberg, 2008).

REFLECTIONS

As a society, we need to realize that our combined efforts can help improve our community's health and well-being. Even though there are numerous cancers that can be prevented, there are segments of our population that do not have the resources to obtain high nutrient-dense foods, to exercise outside on a nice day, to reduce exposure to harmful chemicals that are produced near their homes, or have access to comprehensive health, physical education, and sexuality education in their schools. All of these can help reduce the risk of cancer. Ways to control risk factors include not smoking, limiting exposure to harmful inhalants and chemicals, treating symptoms early, screening and implementing positive lifestyle changes. Each of us has to start within ourselves to improve our health and those around us.

CRITICAL THINKING SKILLS

Level 6, Evaluation. Present and defend opinions by making judgments about information, validity of ideas, or quality of work based on a set of criteria.

Bloom's Taxonomy Key Words. Evaluation, determine, defend, support, explain, conclude, evaluate, rate, and prioritize.

CRITICAL THINKING QUESTIONS

1. What risk factors do you share with family members? Are they external or internal factors?
2. Are you at risk for any cancer primarily caused by external factors? If so, what can you do to reduce your risk?
3. How can society promote, encourage, and support behaviors that reduce the incidence of cancer and improve our well-being? Can some healthy behaviors be more difficult to participate in than others in your community? Why or why not?

WEBSITES

www.cancer.org
American Cancer Society

www.lungusa.org/
American Lung Association

www.livestrong.org/
Live Strong

www.nationalbreastcancer.org/
National Breast Cancer Foundation, Inc.

www.cancer.gov
National Cancer Institute

www.nccc-online.org/
National Cervical Cancer Coalition

www.pcf.org/
Prostate Cancer Foundation

ww5.komen.org/
Susan G. Komen Foundation (breast cancer)

www.testicularcancersociety.org/
Testicular Cancer Society

REFERENCES

American Cancer Society. (2011). *Cancer facts and figures, 2011*. Atlanta, GA: American Cancer Society.

DeVita, T. Jr., Lawrence, T., & Rosenberg S. (eds.). (2008). *Cancer: Principles and practice of oncology*, 8th ed. Philadelphia, PA: Lippincott Williams and Wilkins.

Martin, D., & Gutkind, J. (2009). Human tumor-associated viruses and new insights into the molecular mechanisms of cancer. *Oncogene, 27*, S31–S42.

zur Hausen, H. (2009). Papillomaviruses in the causation of human cancers—A brief historical account. *Virology, 384*, 260–265.